THE STORY OF MANKIND

THE EARTH, ITS WONDERS, ITS SECRETS

THE STORY OF MANKIND

Reader's
Digest

PUBLISHED BY

THE READER'S DIGEST ASSOCIATION LIMITED

LONDON NEW YORK MONTREAL SYDNEY CAPE TOWN

THE STORY OF MANKIND
Edited and designed by Toucan Books, Limited
with Bradbury and Williams
Written by Michael Bright
Edited by Andrew Kerr-Jarrett and Helen Douglas-Cooper
Picture Research by Linda Proud and Christine Vincent

For The Reader's Digest, U.K.
Series Editor Christine Noble
Editorial Assistant Alison Candlin
Editorial Director Cortina Butler
Art Director Nicholas Clark

For The Reader's Digest, U.S.
Series Editor Thomas A. Ranieri
Series Art Editor Martha Grossman
Group Editorial Director Linda Ball

Printed in the United States of America
1998

Address any comments to U.S. Editor, General Books,
260 Madison Ave., New York, NY 10016

Library of Congress Cataloging-in-Publication Data
The story of mankind.
        p.   cm.– (The earth, its wonders, its secrets)
    Includes index.
    ISBN 0-7621-0111-3 (alk. paper)
    1. Human evolution. 2. Prehistoric peoples. 3. Civilization,
Ancient. I. Reader's Digest Association II. Series.
GN281.S86 1998
599.93'8 – dc21   98-18899
                             CIP

Front Cover *Hominid footprints fossilised in volcanic ash
at Laetoli in Tanzania (background). Rock paintings in the San
Francisco mountains, Mexico (inset).*

Page 3 *Aboriginal rock paintings of Wanjana spirit figures.*

CONTENTS

In the Beginning

The story of mankind seems to be linked to the weather, to catastrophes from outer space, and to the violent geological processes that take place within the Earth itself. Whatever the influence, mankind took advantage of every eventuality.

From the very start, the story of life on Earth included some remarkable coincidences. A swirling mass of gases in space gave rise to a system of planets that formed around our own particular star, the Sun. Our planet was just the right distance from the source of energy, consisted of just the right chemicals and developed just the right atmosphere and seas for life as we know it to begin. Through a series of fits and starts a diverse range of creatures evolved which became ever more sophisticated: first, single-celled living things, such as bacteria and algae; then multi-celled creatures ranging eventually from jellyfish to worms, insects to fish, scaled reptiles and feathered birds to furry mammals.

Global catastrophes regularly annihilated large swathes of life on Earth. There was, for example, one extraordinary mass extinction that terminated the Permian period, 250 million years ago, when 96 per cent of all life forms in the oceans disappeared – in other words, almost all the life then existing on the planet. We know this because of fossil evidence locked up in ancient layers of rock – the creatures that existed before 250 million years ago suddenly vanish from the fossil record.

The causes are unknown, although extraterrestrial events are an explanation favoured by many scientists today. Speculation has it that asteroids or comets have regularly collided with the Earth, the impact causing, first, a blow-back of intense heat that cremates any living thing within the immediate vicinity of the impact. Secondly, millions of tons of ash and debris are thrown into the atmosphere where they blot out the life-giving energy of the sun.

Whatever the mechanism of mass extinction, it has helped to keep the animal kingdom fit. The weak, the susceptible and the overspecialised disappear, but the adaptable survive.

PERIODIC CATASTROPHES

Another such disaster took place about 65 million years ago. It wiped out the dominant life forms on the planet – the dinosaurs and their relatives – and left an ecological vacuum which was eventually filled by the rise of the mammals.

Waiting in the trees were the mammals – small creatures, the size and shape of modern-day tree shrews – ancestors of today's humans as well as all other mammal species. They were generalists, more adaptable than the dinosaurs, ready to seize on any opportunity. They evolved, diversified and proliferated, filling the ecological niches vacated by the dinosaurs. By about 55 million years ago, they had given rise to the first primates, the group that now includes monkeys, apes – and humans.

Then, about 25 million years ago, major movements in the plates that make up the

SMALL BEGINNINGS *The modern tree shrew resembles the small, ancient, tree-dwelling mammals that eventually evolved into people.*

Earth's crust forced up new mountain ranges which interrupted the flow of the winds. The climate shifted and thick forests began to thin out. Very gradually, over millions of years after this less devastating, but nevertheless significant change in the weather and vegetation, ape-like creatures started to come down from the trees. At first, they lived partly in the trees, partly on the ground; eventually, during the last 5 million years, they began to live in groups mostly on the grassland floor. They scavenged, hunted and formed social groups. Exposed as they were to all manner of dangers, competing

THE BIRTH OF STARS
Embryonic stars emerge from the Eagle Nebula 7000 light years from Earth. Among them might be another sun and solar system, with the right conditions for life to begin.

DARWIN'S BULLDOG *Biologist Thomas Huxley supported Charles Darwin's notion that mankind had descended from ape-like ancestors.*

with many predators and other scavengers for food, the larger-brained 'thinking' individuals survived and the less clever ones became extinct. Among the survivors some learned to stand up, releasing their hands for other tasks, and the way was clear for tools and weapons to be invented. Eventually these ape-like animals spread throughout the world and evolved into the species that came not only to dominate life on Earth but also to change the course of evolution.

DARWIN'S THEORY

This is the story of mankind as it has emerged since the naturalist Charles Darwin first proposed his theory of evolution in 1859. It was a controversial theory at the time, defying the teachings of the Bible that God created Adam and Eve from whom all people were descended. Indeed, Darwin tried for a long time to avoid publishing it, knowing the sensitivities it would stir. Nevertheless, when his book *On the Origin of Species* did finally appear in the autumn of 1859, it sold out in a day – such was the excitement it generated.

Darwin did not fight his case in public debate. He was a retiring man who avoided if possible the hustle of academic warfare.

Instead, his views were championed by his fellow biologist Thomas Huxley, nicknamed 'Darwin's bulldog'. It was Huxley who took to the platform in a debate with the Bishop of Oxford, Samuel Wilberforce, at a meeting of the British Association of Science in Oxford in 1860. Wilberforce, known as 'Soapy Sam' because of his unctuous manner, was primed by the anti-Darwinists and asked sarcastically if Huxley traced his descent from the apes through his grandfather's or his grandmother's line. Addressing the packed audience of 700 scientists and philosophers, Huxley remarked with disdain that if he had to choose for an ancestor between an ape or an educated man who could introduce such a question into a serious scientific discussion, he would choose the ape.

In fact, Darwin and Huxley were not the first people to run into trouble for their controversial views about mankind's distant prehistory. Several years earlier, in 1838, the French archaeologist Jacques Boucher de Crévecoeur de Perthes had found some ancient stone axes in Abbeville in northern

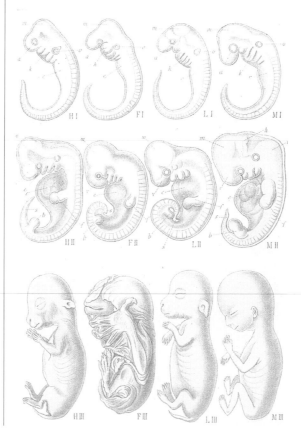

France. In 1846, he published a book on his findings. He asserted that the axes must be thousands of years old and were clearly made by man. The book was greeted with protests. French scientific circles were still dominated by the influence of the zoologist Baron Georges Cuvier, who had died a few years earlier. He had acknowledged that fossils in general were ancient but, as a firm believer in divine creation, he asserted that man could not be. Boucher had found the first evidence of Stone Age man, but the scientific community would not listen.

Signs that the tide of opinion was beginning to turn in favour of the new views came in the 1860s. In 1863 Huxley published a highly influential book based on Darwin's theories, *Man's Place in Nature*. Another book published that year was by the eminent British geologist Sir Charles Lyell and entitled *The Antiquity of Man*. Using Boucher's stone axes as evidence, Lyell argued that man or man-like creatures must have existed on Earth for many thousands of years. Finally, in 1871, Darwin published his own 700 page 'essay' which applied the theory of evolution specifically to mankind, *The Descent of Man*.

EVIDENCE OF BAD DESIGN

The modern study of the story of mankind relies heavily on evidence provided by the fossils of our evolutionary forebears. Darwin, when he was writing *The Descent of Man*, knew of few such fossils. Instead, he had to argue his case in a more roundabout way. He noted, for example, that people and apes are susceptible to the same parasites and diseases, and argued from that to suggest that they are related. Similarly, the human appendix and muscles of the ear no longer serve a purpose –

EMBRYO DEVELOPMENT *Comparison of the embryos of a dog, a bat, a hare and a human shows the same fish-like stage in all of them.*

GIBRALTAR MAN *This skull, found in Gibraltar, is classified as Neanderthal. It was found in 1848, before the skull found in the Neander Valley.*

evidence, he maintained, that humans are descended from creatures in which they did serve a purpose. He even argued that the human embryo, with fish-like gill slits and what looks like a tail, revealed traces of its far distant ancestry among sea creatures.

Since his time, modern science has suggested similar clues to our evolutionary past – notably in some examples of bad design. For example, our ancestry among creatures that walked on four legs is evident in a strip of muscle supporting the intestines. It is correctly constructed and positioned for an animal walking on all fours, but in the upright position it is placed under considerable strain. The result can be a rupture of the tissue and a hernia.

Tortuous though Darwin's original arguments were, they attracted some support from other scientists. The German zoologist Ernst Haeckel even proposed that a creature, which he named '*Pithecanthropus*' (apeman), must have existed as a 'missing link' between apes and modern man.

In fact, the skull of an ancient hominid (or man-like creature) had been found in 1848 in Gibraltar, but it was ignored at the time. Another skull was unearthed in a quarry in the Neander Valley, near Düsseldorf in Germany in 1856, but many scientists considered that it had belonged to a diseased modern human. Only later was it widely accepted that the skull came from an extinct species of human living during the late Pleistocene age (ending around 10 000 years ago). The term Neanderthal was coined to describe it.

It was not until much later again that more fossil evidence began to appear that was widely accepted by the scientific community. A key figure was the Dutch doctor Eugène Dubois who gave up his university post in order to search for the missing link. In 1891, he was with the Royal Dutch East Indies Army in Java when he discovered the skull cap and thigh bone of a hominid that had stood erect. It was given the scientific name '*Pithecanthropus erectus*', meaning 'the erect apeman'. Some people believed that Dubois had found the missing link, but in the years that followed it became clear that there was not simply a single missing link but an entire evolutionary series bridging the millennia between ape-like hominids and modern man.

More fossils followed. In 1908 a full Neanderthal skeleton was found in south-west France. In 1924 the skull of the so-called 'southern ape' was unearthed from a cave site in South Africa and later publicised by the anatomist Raymond Dart. In 1959 'Nutcracker man' – so-named because of its powerful jaws – was discovered in Tanzania by the anthropologist Louis Leakey and his wife Mary, and in 1978 the footprints of a hominid that walked upright 3.7 million years ago were found, also in Tanzania, by Mary Leakey. In the past few decades, fossil bones of early men have been uncovered in many parts of the world: in the region of Lake Turkana, Koobi Fora and the Omo river, Kenya; in Olduvai Gorge and Laetoli, Tanzania; in the Afar Depression, Ethiopia; in the Petralona

TURKANA *At excavations at Lake Turkana in northern Kenya Richard Leakey, son of Louis and Mary, found many important hominid fossils.*

Cave of northern Greece; in the Siwalik Hills in Pakistan; and at Sterkfontein and Makapansgat in southern Africa.

The Fossil Jigsaw

The early story of mankind lasts from the time ancestral ape-men came down from the trees to the time when human beings as we know ourselves grew crops, built cities, studied the heavens, painted pictures and travelled the world.

Clues to this story survive in fossil bones and in preserved living sites and artefacts, including ancient jewellery and works of art (such as cave paintings), unearthed by archaeologists. But piecing the clues together is a complex task. We are often left with no more than a few fragments – of fossilised bone, say – or a single tooth. Yet even from such meagre evidence a picture can be re-created. A small piece of jaw, for example, may give some clues to the size of an animal's teeth, the shape of its mouth and the size and power of its jaw muscles. This, in turn, offers clues about the size and shape of its face and head. From this we may be able to guess what it ate, and therefore the kind of environment it lived in. Knowing this indicates the other animals with which it shared its living space, including predators and prey. If the food is thought to include meat, it may also be possible to guess whether the animal hunted alone or in a group – large prey would have to be hunted in a group. If the animal hunted in a group, it must have had social rules. All this is derived from a piece of archaic jaw bone.

But how did the fossilised debris get there in the first place? Like so much else

that relates to the story of mankind, fossil formation depends heavily on chance: an ancient creature must have died at just the right time and at just the right place for fossilisation to occur. An animal or plant must

VIOLENT EARTH *Volcanic ash regularly smothered mankind's early ancestors, providing the volcanic rock used to date fossil finds today.*

be buried rapidly, since it will rot if it is exposed too long to the air. A hungry hyena, for example, with its robust teeth and powerful jaws, could easily demolish a carcass, bones and all, thus destroying any evidence of its existence. Bones also disintegrate quickly when they are exposed to hot sun and torrential rain. The soft parts of an animal or plant are rarely preserved, except when they are smothered rapidly after death or when the plant or animal is buried alive. Sudden volcanic eruptions are particularly useful preservers, to the extent that they even sometimes preserve the soft parts. A site near Lake Victoria in East Africa is a witness to this, with insects, spiders, roots and leaves embalmed in the rocks in the finest detail.

One of the most fruitful sources of fossils is the Great Rift Valley of East Africa, an area of weakness in the Earth's crust. When mankind's ancestors were undergoing the remarkable change from ape to human, the Great Rift was undergoing a transformation of its own. What had been no more than a shallow depression, marked by lakes and volcanoes some 20 million years ago, was becoming a deep rift, lined with escarpments and violent volcanoes. The landscape was blanketed from time to time with volcanic ash, and the rivers and lakes came and went. Living things were engulfed and preserved, and as a consequence the Great Rift Valley has today become a mecca for scientists studying the origins of humanity.

Imagine the scene many thousands of years ago. One of our ancestors staggers to the lakeside, collapses and dies – early hominids, like people today, would have had water, a river or a lake, as a focus for their everyday lives. The corpse then attracts scavengers, such as jackals and vultures, which pull the body apart, remove the soft parts and scatter many of the bones. The remains are picked over by beetles, flies and grubs, and are then buried slowly by river and lake sediments. In a volcanically active region like the Great Rift Valley, the entire area is covered with ash from a nearby active volcano, and as layer upon layer of ash and sediment gradually, over thousands of years, piles up, the rubble undergoes chemical and physical change. The sediments become what are known as sedimentary rocks, while water-soluble minerals go to work on the bone, transforming it, often molecule by molecule, into stone. In this way, a fossil is formed.

RICHES UNEARTHED

The fossils, by this time, are buried deep in the earth and inaccessible to all except coal miners and mineral prospectors – which is why so many key fossils, giving us crucial insights into the story of mankind, have been found in quarries and mines. But they can also become uncovered naturally. Major earth movements push up the layers of rock, bringing the fossil-bearing beds to the surface. In the Himalayan foothills, where the sedimentary rocks are 20 000 ft (6100 m) thick, strata containing the fossils of ancient apes have been exposed in the Siwalik Hills in Pakistan. And in the 25 mile (40 km) long Olduvai Gorge in Tanzania, where a river has cut a 300 ft (90 m) deep gash through the arid landscape, scientists are presented with a layer cake of fossil-bearing strata alternating with datable layers of volcanic ash.

The problem for scientists is in building up a complete picture from the fossils presented to them in this way. The chances of any animal becoming a fossil in the first place are not great, and the chances of a fossil being found hundreds, thousands or millions of years later are even less.

Fossilised debris, found in sediments that also contain hominid remains, is useful in establishing the date of the layer and the conditions at the time. Even in the absence of easily identifiable plant remnants, pollen grains – each species sporting its distinctive outer coat – will indicate the vegetation of the time. Traces of other animals also offer clues. The presence of fish and hippo bones, crocodile teeth and shells tells us that there was a lake. A preponderance of antelope bones indicates savannah conditions, whereas a glut of monkey remains points to a forest. The rocks themselves have a story to tell. Rock formed from the thick, fine-grained silt or mud at the bottom of a lake or pond, for example, looks quite different from that formed from the coarse-grained sand at the bottom of a fast-flowing river.

In some parts of the world, such as southern Africa and Greece, human origins are associated with quite different geological processes. While fossils in the East African Rift are found spread out over areas measured in hundreds of square miles, elsewhere they may be found on sites no more than a few yards across, such as caves. Caves, carved out of limestone rocks by rivers and streams in upland areas and by waves on the seashore, have long been invaded by animals (including early humans) seeking refuge from the weather and predators. Fossils lie in the rubble on the cave floor, and are incorporated in the coarse sedimentary rocks which form there. Each epoch of occupancy accumulates its own layer of bones, debris and in-fill and so the cave gradually fills up like a layer-cake.

Caves also contain concentrations of ancient human 'litter', such as the leftovers from a meal, a broken pot or a discarded arrowhead. From these, scientists are able to reconstruct parts of our ancestors' way of

FOSSIL TREASURE TROVE
Erosion by wind and rain
exposes the fossils that have
been locked up inside
sedimentary rocks.

life. Pottery, statuettes, ornaments and cave paintings give them clues about culture, religion and art, while butchering implements and weapons offer insights into technology.

GENETIC IMPRINTS

In recent decades, a new way of exploring the distant past has emerged, through the study of DNA – the blueprint of life contained in every animal and plant cell. This enables scientists to follow our family tree back to our distant ancestors. By studying the DNA of modern populations of humans, animals and plants, they can work out who is, or was, related to whom – which animals share the same genetic characteristics and which are very different. They can also suggest a timescale during which the evolutionary process that created the difference happened, the so-called 'molecular clock'.

Evolution may be gradual, the result of mutations and changing environmental

ANCIENT PICTURES Early people were not always fighting or feeding, but had time to paint pictures, like this one from Mexico, of the creatures they saw around them.

STUFF OF LIFE A computer simulation of a DNA molecule. DNA is the blueprint of life, carrying genetic information from one generation to the next.

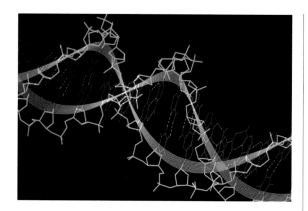

influences. Alternatively, it may be that long periods of relative evolutionary stability are punctuated by the comparatively sudden appearance of a new species. No one is sure which is correct. Evolution also seems to take place in a mosaic fashion – some parts of an organism change more rapidly than others. One thing is certain, however. Any change leaves its mark in the DNA, and it can be traced through time.

The idea of using the DNA molecule as an evolutionary clock rests on a single assumption. Once two species separate in evolution, the genetic material in the two lines accumulates changes or mutations – the longer the separation, the more the changes. If the rate at which these changes occur remains steady (and there is considerable debate about this), and if you can measure the differences between two species, you can also measure the time that has elapsed

since they derived from a common ancestor.

In studying the evolution of humans and our genetic relationship with the other great apes, the calculations show that modern humans have changed by only 1 to 2 per cent from modern apes, and that the split took place between 5 and 10 million years ago.

The tale of our origins is, in reality, an extraordinary detective story, full of clues, red herrings, blind alleys and uncertainties. Dedicated scientific sleuths attempt to piece together the evidence, consisting very often of tiny, unrelated fragments of prehistory, in order to create a meaningful account of our time on Earth. As a species, we are comparative latecomers, and scientists have a hard time studying our earliest beginnings because the fossil record is so poor. Nevertheless, palaeontologists (scientists who study fossils), archaeologists (scientists who study the cultural remains and monuments of the past), and palaeoanthropologists (scientists who study the remains of early man) have painstakingly collected and assimilated the evidence. Their hypotheses are rarely accepted immediately by their peers and contemporaries, and are often controversial. In this field of scientific endeavour, reputations have been won and lost on a single fossil find, and intellectual friends have turned to sworn enemies overnight. It is, after all, a very personal story, our own story – the story of mankind.

THE EMERGENCE OF MAN

1

SOUTH AFRICAN BABY *The Taung skull is from a three-year-old gracile 'ape-man'.*

THE STORY OF MAN'S EMERGENCE STARTS WITH CAT-SIZED CREATURES THAT LIVED SOME 37 MILLION YEARS AGO AND FINISHES, AROUND 40 000 YEARS AGO, WITH CRO-MAGNON MAN, MODERN *HOMO SAPIENS,* WHO CREATED SUCH MASTERPIECES AS THE CAVE PAINTINGS OF LES EYZIES IN FRANCE AND ALTAMIRA IN SPAIN. IT IS A COMPLEX STORY THAT MODERN SCIENTISTS HAVE STILL NOT MANAGED TO UNRAVEL. CERTAIN THINGS ARE CLEAR, HOWEVER. OUR DISTANT FOREBEARS GREW IN SIZE AND LEARNED TO WALK UPRIGHT. LIFE BECAME MORE COMPLEX AND DEMANDED LARGER BRAINS. FROM BEING HERBIVORES,

COUSINS *Modern humans have many predecessors.*

THEY BECAME OMNIVORES — FIRST SCAVENGING AND THEN HUNTING PREY. FINALLY, MODERN MAN EMERGED AND SET OUT TO CONQUER THE WORLD.

THE DAWN APE

One of the earliest-known apes was no bigger than a large domestic cat. Aegyptopithecus *lived about 37-32 million years ago in the tropical rain forests and wetlands that then spread out across much of North Africa and the Middle East.*

In a part of Africa with a landscape more reminiscent of Mars than Earth, fossil hunters from Duke University in the United States are finding the fossilised remains of the earliest higher primates. These are the possible forerunners of both the great apes and man. The fossils are in rocks dating from the period in the Earth's history known as the Oligocene epoch – 38 to 25 million years ago. A few have been found nearby that are even older.

The place is the hot, dry desert of Egypt's El Faiyum Depression, 62 miles (100 km) south-west of Cairo on the edge of the Sahara. More than 33 million years ago, it was a quite different place: the climate of North Africa and the Middle East was wetter and the depression was filled with the lush vegetation of a tropical rain forest crisscrossed by numerous broad, meandering rivers that flowed into the Mediterranean. Fossil plant remains of mangroves, vines and water lilies are found there, as are intact fossil tree trunks more than 50 yd (46 m) long.

The fossilised remains of water birds suggest large areas of open, shallow freshwater lakes and ponds containing rafts of floating vegetation. Jaçanas with long toes walked on lilypads, and shoebill storks foraged on dense mats of floating weeds from which they captured large fish in their massive bills by breaking through the vegetation. Fossil cormorants, rails, herons and flamingos provide further evidence that the place was dominated by water. Such a habitat today exists in Uganda, in a region of swampland bordered by forests and grasslands to the north and west of Lake Victoria. This area is inhabited by the modern counterparts of the fossilised El Faiyum birds – suggesting that this small part of Africa may resemble the environment in which the ancestors of man lived.

The monsoon-like conditions that prevailed in El Faiyum, with permanently damp soils and periodic sea flooding, were not, on the face of things, conducive to fossil formation. Nevertheless, a wealth of fossil bones from birds, reptiles, fish and mammals have been found in a 1100 ft (340 m) thick layer of sandstone, mudstone, conglomerate and limestone rocks that was formed from these ancient low-lying, swamp-forest lands. A layer of basaltic rock (dense, dark volcanic rock) caps the fossil beds. The topmost lava flows

ANCIENT ANCESTOR
Aegyptopithecus, *a tree-dweller, had grasping hands and feet and ran on all fours.*

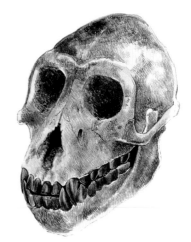

EARLY CLUES Aegyptopithecus *had a primitively long snout, but its bony, protective eye sockets are a feature shared by all the higher primates.*

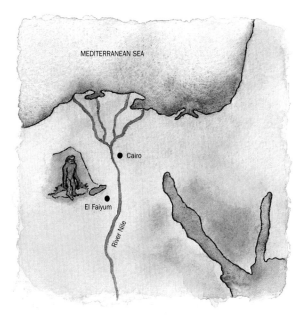

MEDITERRANEAN SEA

Cairo

El Faiyum

River Nile

EARLY FINDS *Aegyptopithecus was found at a site at El Faiyum in Egypt.*

sockets, giving better protection than in many other animals, and the teeth share features with modern apes and man. A crest on top of the skull, known as the sagittal crest, would have anchored unusually large jaw muscles, a feature common in animals that have evolved from smaller ancestors – the gorilla is a modern example. As the body grows bigger over the generations, the creature has to develop heavier jaws and more powerful jaw muscles to feed the larger body. The crest gives *Aegyptopithecus* a resemblance to the larger ape-like creatures that followed in the fossil record – *Sivapithecus, Proconsul, Dryopithecus*, the robust *Australopithecus* and modern day male orang-utans.

The creature's snout was short and the brain larger in proportion to body size than in any other primate known to be living at that time. Each fossil skull has shown facial differences and different brain sizes, even though they are thought to come from the same species. All this suggests that individuals might have been able to recognise each other. If that was the case, it makes it possible that they lived in large groups. Big groups need social hierarchies to prevent strife as large numbers of individuals compete for food. These are possible only if the members of the group can

HEAD BABOON *Male olive baboons indicate their status in the group by showing their large canine teeth in a gesture resembling a yawn.*

recognise each other. Living in larger groups would have been a significant advance on more primitive primates living in smaller groups where individuality was less obvious.

There is evidence that dominant members of the large groups were males. Some of the canine teeth unearthed so far are relatively small and probably served purely for eating; experts assume that these belonged to females. Canine teeth probably coming from males are larger, fang-like and more obvious. In the way that male baboons 'yawn' and show their large canines, dawn ape males most likely bared their teeth in aggressive, threatening displays to show which one was the boss ape. From jaw sizes, it is thought that the males were bigger than the females, the males weighing about 10-11 lb (4.5-5

have been dated to 26 million years ago, while those at the bottom of the layer are 31 million years old. The fossils found in rocks below the basalt are older still, having been laid down about 33 million years ago.

In more recent years, winds and flash floods have scoured the desert sediments, eroding the rocks and uncovering the fossilised remains of what may be one of man's earliest-known ancestors *Aegyptopithecus zeuxis*, the 'dawn ape', living from about 37 to 32 million years ago. Several incomplete skeletons, jaws and teeth, and a small skull, have been discovered, the fossil evidence enabling scientists to speculate about the size, shape and lifestyle of this early primate.

ROOTS IN AFRICA

Aegyptopithecus was about the size of a large domestic cat. It had a long, sinuous back and long limbs, and superficially resembled a modern Madagascan lemur. It had grasping fingers and toes, indicating not only a tree-dwelling lifestyle, but also that it was capable of bringing food, most probably fruits and nuts, to its mouth. In fact, the fossilised pinecone-like fruits of *Epipremnum* – a climbing vine still found in South-east Asia – have been found in the rock layers containing the bone fragments. It is thought they were an important part of the *Aegyptopithecus* diet.

The skull and jaws of the dawn ape show advanced features, including enclosed eye

A MODEL FOR THE COMMON ANCESTOR OF APES AND HUMANS

Apes and humans share a common ancestor. But what did this creature look like? And is there any species living today that resembles it in significant ways? Using allometry – a technique that analyses how the shape of the body changes as its overall size alters – Leslie Aiello at University College, London, has indeed proposed a modern-day model for our common ancestor.

The great apes have manipulative hands and are adapted to climbing trees; modern humans also have manipulative hands but stand upright. All these – the manipulative hands, the ability to climb trees or walk upright – are specialist adaptations equipping us to survive in our particular habitats. Any modern-day model for our forebear must have a body form which could be modified into such specialist developments.

Among modern creatures that rules out chimpanzees, gibbons, orang-utans and Old World monkeys which are already too specialised. There is, however, a New World monkey that has the right qualities: the howler monkey of Central and South America. Like *Aegyptopithecus*, the howler is heavy-boned, indicating that it is deliberate in its movements. Indeed, it proceeds by 'slow climbing', using all four limbs in such a way that the forelimbs rarely take the body's full weight. This is important: it means that its body form could be modified over millennia to upright walking where the hindlimbs take the weight. A similar creature could have been the ancestor of humans. Equally, the howler monkey can also move about underneath branches, in the manner of many apes, rather than on top of them like Old World monkeys. This qualifies a similar creature to be an ancestor of the apes. On the other hand, an ancestor of apes and humans would probably not have had a prehensile tail as howlers do.

This possible similarity between the howler monkey and our common ancestor is not, however, a result of genetic closeness. It is simply a question of similar adaptations to a common tropical rain-forest habitat.

LIKE OUR FOREBEAR *With the exception of its prehensile tail, the howler monkey may well resemble the common ancestor of apes and humans.*

LIFE IN THE TREES *The gibbon has the long, strong forelimbs of a tree-dweller that gets about by swinging from branch to branch.*

kg), the females 8-9 lb (3.6-4 kg). The larger males would have fought for the right to mate and defended the group from predators just as modern male apes and monkeys do.

Curious puncture marks, discovered on skull, jaw and limb bones suggest that these creatures fell prey to early mammalian carnivores known as creodonts, the ancestors of modern cats and dogs.

OUR FOREBEARS' FOREBEARS

Experts cannot yet prove that *Aegyptopithecus* was on the direct line to man, though they are confident that it at least resembled the early ancestors of man and apes. But who were the ancestors of *Aegyptopithecus* and others like it? In 1983, the team at El Faiyum discovered part of the lower jaw of an even earlier primate that lived 40 million years ago. The tiny creature, at 11 oz (300 g), was no larger than a marmoset and a quarter of the size of the smallest living Old World monkey. It was dubbed *Qatrania wingi*. It probably lived on a vegetable diet, mainly of fruit, with the occasional snack of insects. It was, in 1983, the earliest-known anthropoid – the group that includes monkeys, apes and humans.

Then, in 1992, French and Algerian scientists unearthed a collection of teeth in Algeria. These, found in deposits between 50 and 46 million years old, they attributed to an even more ancient anthropoid. They called it *Algeripithecus minutus* on account of its size: the living animal could have been no more than 5-11 oz (150-300 g), the size of a dwarf bush baby. Its teeth resemble those of *Aegyptopithecus*, but there are so few of them that experts are reluctant to agree that this creature is a significant discovery. If it is, however, and the rocks in which the teeth were found are really 50-46 million years old, it pushes back considerably – possibly to 60 million years ago – the date at which the anthropoids emerged as a distinct branch of the primate family tree.

The fossil record yields evidence of two other branches. The omomyids were most probably nocturnal, ate fruit and insects and are thought to have given rise to modern-day tarsiers. The adapids were larger than the omomyids, probably diurnal, and ate fruit and leaves; they gave rise to the lemurs and lorises. Fossil evidence indicates that the adapids moved north into Europe about 53 million years ago when the climate there became warmer. They also moved south in Africa, where the lemurs became isolated on Madagascar. The omomyids moved into Asia, where they diversified, with one branch heading on to North America. The anthropoids diversified in Africa, moving into Asia about 45 million years ago.

Until the Algerian find, both omomyids and adapids had been put forward as possible common ancestors of the anthropoids – monkeys, apes and men. But most omomyid and adapid fossil bones and teeth have been found in Europe and North America in rocks dated at between 50 and 30 million years old. If the Algerian finds are as old as they seem, the European and North American omomyids and adapids would be contemporary with *Algeripithecus*, and therefore eliminated from the story of the origins of mankind.

HANDS AND EYES

When the earliest primates took to the trees, anatomical changes took place that would have great significance in the story of mankind. They needed grasping hands for moving about safely and quickly in the branches, and stereoscopic eyesight – with eyes at the front rather than the sides of the head – to focus on insect prey. Sitting upright freed their hands to manipulate food. These changes also meant that they were having to process more and more information. As a result, their brains had to adapt by increasing in size.

The most important change in the primate forelimb is the evolution from a clawed paw to a hand with separate and movable fingers, an opposable thumb and a precision grip. The grip, in which the thumb and index finger meet, has enabled higher primates to pick up and manipulate small objects, such as food, weapons and tools. The opposable thumb, in which the thumb can be moved across the palm of the hand, is best developed in humans, but many other higher primates possess it to some extent. New World monkeys bring thumb and index finger together in a scissor-like action, while Old World monkeys bring the tips together with some success. The chimpanzee, which uses the back of its hand for knuckle walking, presses its thumb to the side of its bent finger, but can none the less fashion twigs for such finely tuned behaviour as 'termite fishing'.

The small, early primates were probably nocturnal animals with large

eyes, but as they evolved into larger diurnal (day-living) creatures, the complex network of optic nerves at the back of the eyes was adapted for colour vision. The ability to see in colour helped the animal to discriminate objects on a single-colour background. In their forest home, the early primates saw everything against the green of the

HANDS UP *From left to right: The chimpanzee, gorilla and baboon have hands adapted to picking up and holding objects, but only humans are capable of a precision grip.*

ATTRACTED TO COLOUR *Stereoscopic colour vision enables a chimpanzee to spot a prize for which it was worth getting wet.*

forest canopy, so being able to pick out an occasional splash of colour, such as a fruit or a juicy insect, was a useful progression.

It was the ability to see a three-dimensional world in colour that the forest-living primates took with them when they came down from the trees. It gave them a distinct advantage over the ground-living animals with which they were about to compete.

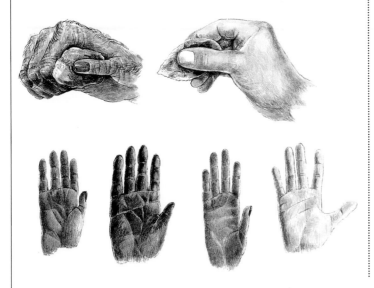

AN INCOMPLETE STORY

The story of mankind is short and incomplete. As told by modern experts, it is one of fact mixed with imaginative guesswork. Fossils of ancient ape-like and human-like beings offer us glimpses of our prehistory, but the finds are sporadic in time, geographically widespread, and often incomplete. Genetic studies, in which modern-day wizards tap into the principles of biological inheritance, attempt to trace back our hereditary lines. Sometimes these agree with the fossil-hunters' findings; other times they do not.

That we are primates – members of the biological order that ranges from us to the prosimians (lemurs, lorises and tarsiers), typically possessing dextrous hands and feet and binocular vision – there is no doubt. We are also anthropoids, members of the primate suborder that includes monkeys, apes and humans. Our distant cousins, the monkeys, distinguished by having tails, include the New World monkeys (such as the marmosets of the Americas) and the Old World monkeys (such as the baboons of Africa and Arabia). Our closer relatives are the apes – tailless, unlike the monkeys – such as the chimpanzees, gorillas and orang-utans.

The stages of our development, and the timing on the family tree of our breakaway from our ape-like cousins, are less precise. The story appears to have been one of fits and starts – periods of rapid evolution interspersed with intervals of stability. There was, for example, a long and slow development during the Miocene, starting 23 million years ago, which ended with a sudden – in evolutionary terms – spurt of growth from the Pliocene, starting 5 million years ago, until about 10 000 years ago. Once the rapidly evolving human brain began to register the advantages of tools and weapons, fire, cooperative hunting and sharing of resources, there was no holding it back. Eventually early *Homo sapiens* emerged and so the story of the modern human race bagan.

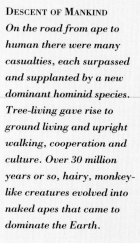

Aegyptopithecus

OLIGOCENE

26 million years ago

Proconsul

MIOCENE

BRAINY PEOPLE *The evolution of humans is closely linked to the development of the human brain, a feature readily visible in the skulls of our ancestors and ourselves. A small-brained progenitor eventually evolved, through a series of stages, into the large-brained, flat-faced individuals we recognise as humans.*

DESCENT OF MANKIND
On the road from ape to human there were many casualties, each surpassed and supplanted by a new dominant hominid species. Tree-living gave rise to ground living and upright walking, cooperation and culture. Over 30 million years or so, hairy, monkey-like creatures evolved into naked apes that came to dominate the Earth.

7 million years ago

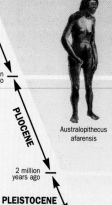
Australopithecus afarensis

2 million years ago

PLIOCENE

PLEISTOCENE

10 000 years ago

Australopithecus africanus

Homo habilis

Homo erectus

Neanderthal

Cro-Magnon man

LANDS OF OUR FATHERS *Fossil remains of our earliest forebears have all been found in Africa, at sites such as Hadar in modern Ethiopia. Later ancestors, such as Homo erectus and the Neanderthals, were well spread across the Old World.*

LOCATION OF FOSSIL FINDS

1. Swanscombe
2. Neander Valley
3. Cro-Magnon
4. Gibraltar
5. Monte Circeo
6. Petralona
7. Salé
8. Tighennif
9. Quafzeh
10. Shanidar
11. Teshik-Tash
12. Narmada
13. Jinniu Shan
14. Lantian
15. Hexian
16. Java
17. Yayo
18. Hadar
19. Turkana
20. Olduvai Gorge
21. Taung
22. Saldanha

THE FAMILY OF MAN

Lemurs and Lorises

Tarsiers

New World Monkeys

Old World Monkeys

Gibbons

Orang-utans

Gorillas

Chimpanzees

Humans

EVOLUTION OF THE PRIMATES *Many attempts have been made to construct an accurate evolutionary tree for mankind and its relatives, but the paucity of fossils makes it difficult to be definite. This tree shows man's distant relationship with lemurs, tarsiers and monkeys, and close links with the apes. It proposes that the closest relative of humans is the chimpanzee.*

PROCONSUL AND FRIENDS

Apes flourished in the forests that covered much of Africa, Europe and Asia from about 20 to 10 million years ago, and many – such as the baboon-sized Proconsul *– have at some time been proposed as candidates for the 'missing link'.*

The Miocene epoch, which spanned the period from 24 to 5 million years ago, remains mysterious, chiefly because mankind's descent is poorly represented in the fossil record. But from the available evidence, it is clear that the Miocene was a time of great environmental change during which our forebears had to adapt or disappear. It was a period when the ancestral lines of modern orang-utans, gorillas and chimpanzees and humans went their separate ways. How and when these important events occurred, however, has not been established.

The primates of the early Miocene, from 20 to 18 million years ago, like those in the preceding Oligocene epoch, flourished in thick tropical forests, but many of those in the middle Miocene were confronted with less dense, temperate to tropical woodland. Gaps between the stands of trees meant that the tree-dwelling apes had to walk from one thicket to another. Exclusively tree-dwelling animals needed to become partly terrestrial.

In woodlands, fruits were less abundant and more seasonal than in tropical forests and so our formerly vegetarian ancestors had to change their diet. They became omnivorous, eating both meat and plants, and the switch in habitat and food was marked by significant anatomical adaptations. Changes in the muscles of the face and skull, such as those involved in chewing, were to persist through to modern man and in the evolution of our relatives, the great apes.

The woodland belt stretched from West Africa to south-western China, from southern Africa to central and southern Europe. The leaves on the trees were small, evergreen and leathery, enabling the plants to survive during the hot, dry seasons of a Mediterranean-type climate. The woodlands were sandwiched between tropical and sub-tropical forests stretching towards the Equator and wet temperate forests of mixed conifers and broad-leaved deciduous trees towards the poles. Ape-like ancestors lived in all three forest and woodland belts.

PROCONSULAR APES

One ape-like being living in the tropical forests was the creature known as *Proconsul*. The first remains of *Proconsul* were found by the palaeontologists Louis and Mary Leakey in 1948 on Rusinga Island in Lake Victoria

ANCIENT SKULL *The skull of* Proconsul, *which lived about 18 million years ago, shows the jutting, chimpanzee-like face.*

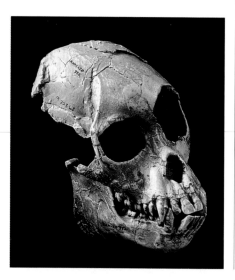

EARLY APE *The tree-dwelling* Proconsul *was larger than a monkey, and displayed a combination of monkey and ape-like features.*

in East Africa. Louis Leakey was excavating a fossil crocodile skeleton and his wife went walking to look for something more stimulating. Her attention was first drawn to a tooth poking out of the soil, and on closer inspection she found jaws and facial bones. Eventually half a skull was excavated, together with some foot and leg bones.

Many years later, a palaeontologist was rummaging through a box, labelled 'Rusinga 1947', that mostly contained fossil turtle shells, when he spotted some pieces of skull. It turned out that the fragments were not any old fossils of *Proconsul*, but were the pieces missing from the Leakeys' *Proconsul* skull. A team had chanced upon them the year before Mary Leakey made her find but had missed the vital fragments. Encouraged by this find, scientists have searched all the Rusinga boxes and have found enough limb bones, vertebrae and shoulder blades to rebuild most of the skeleton.

Proconsul was a tailless branch-walker – it climbed along branches rather than swinging from them. It was roughly the size of a modern baboon, and lived some 18 million

BONE FRAGMENTS *Leg bones, jaw bones and teeth from* **Ramapithecus,** *an ancestor of the orang-utan, date back 15 million years.*

years ago. Its features were a curious mixture of monkey and ape: a long monkey-like body with monkey-like arms and hands, but ape-like shoulders and elbows and a large ape-like head. It probably ran along branches on all fours like modern monkeys and ate soft fruits. Males were larger than females.

CANDIDATES FOR THE MISSING LINK

For a while, *Proconsul* was considered a likely candidate for the 'missing link' between apes and man. However, many other ape-like creatures have been unearthed, many of which are also good candidates. One that was living about the same time as *Proconsul*

was championed in the 1970s. It was given the scientific name *Ramapithecus brevirostris*, meaning 'Rama's short-faced ape', after the Hindu god; the first fossil – a fragment of upper jaw – was found in India in 1932. Since then many more bones have been found in Pakistan, China, Greece, Turkey, Hungary and East Africa, and scientists have been able to piece together an ancient creature about the size of a modern gibbon. Its jaws were sturdy, its canine teeth small (nearly the same size in male and females) and its cheek teeth or molars were capped with thick enamel – all features that led many scientists to believe it was a direct ancestor of mankind.

Robust jaws with well-worn teeth suggested that *Ramapithecus* consumed nuts and hard fruits and probably lived mainly in the trees where these were to be found in plenty. But a specimen discovered in Africa in 1962, which was first given the name *Kenyapithecus* but later considered to resemble closely the Asian *Ramapithecus*, was

FOREST-DWELLER
The subtropical evergreen forests of China provided one of the homes of the Asian Ramapithecus.

BUSH BABIES AND EARLY PRIMATE SOCIETIES

Scientists in southern Africa have fitted tiny radio transmitters to bush babies and then followed individual animals using radio-tracking equipment. It used to be thought that bush babies lived in small family groups, but the results of the new field work showed that this was wrong.

Previously, researchers had found bush babies huddled together in day nests and assumed that they were related, but the radio-tracking experiments revealed that each day the nest could include different individuals. It turns out that bush babies and several other nocturnal primates have a female group as their basic social unit. This consists of several females and their offspring. A day nest contains females whose home ranges overlap. Male ranges interlock with those of the females,

the larger, dominant males having access to the females and the smaller 'satellite' males denied the right to mate. Although bush babies appear to forage alone at night, they do in fact communicate regularly with others of their kind and extensively scent mark their sleeping trees. They sleep in groups but do not move around in groups.

It is possible that the social systems of most monkeys, apes and even man could be derived from this basic nocturnal social system of female groups. For example, the harem system of baboons may have evolved when males started to move around with female groups by day. The multi-male system of vervet monkeys may have evolved when peripheral males were allowed in to join the group, and the family grouping, common to humans, could be

achieved if the number of females to a single male was restricted to one.

So, it seems that the modern bush baby, a relatively primitive primate, might offer a model of the way that ape and human societies evolved from a basic ancestral pattern.

BUSH BABY SOCIETY Female bush babies from local territories gather together with their young during the day. It is possible that these bands represent the basic primate social unit.

found in geological beds more reminiscent of savannah with isolated stands of woodland. *Ramapithecus*, it seems, was already making forays down from the trees, and had turned to seed and root-eating like modern-day gelada baboons.

Ramapithecus survived on Earth from about 14 to 8 million years ago, a very long time in anthropological terms. If, however, it was a direct ancestor of man, this time span would mean that the branch of the evolutionary tree leading to humankind split from the rest of the animal kingdom about 16 million years ago. Most palaeoanthropologists now consider this date to be far too

early. During the past 20 years the evidence supporting *Ramapithecus* as our ancestor, or even its existence as a single species, has gradually been eroded. The ancient creature that now takes centre stage is *Sivapithecus*.

SIVAPITHECUS, ORANG-UTANS AND HUMANS

Sivapithecus is another ape of the Miocene. The first specimen was discovered in Asia in 1910; others were found in India, Pakistan and Turkey. It seems that the sivapithecines survived for a long time. The oldest specimen so far discovered, in Turkey, probably lived 15-14 million years ago. Fossil bones of what are

considered to be several different species have been found across Europe and Asia, including some from more recent strata dated just 7.5 million years ago.

Sivapithecus was a tree-dwelling, fruit-eating animal about the size of a chimpanzee but with a face that resembles southern Asia's last-remaining ape, the orang-utan. Experts rule out more recent sivapithecines as candidates for the common ancestor of apes and humans, because of their relatively young age and their remoteness from later hominid finds in east and southern Africa. Earlier species of *Sivapithecus*, however, could have been our ancestors – or close to them. The creature could have arisen in Africa and spread to Europe and Asia at a time 16 million or so years ago when the continent of

FAMILY LIKENESS The skulls of the orang-utan (far left) and Sivapithecus (centre) share features of early hominid stock, such as the shape of the eye socket, not found in the chimpanzee (left).

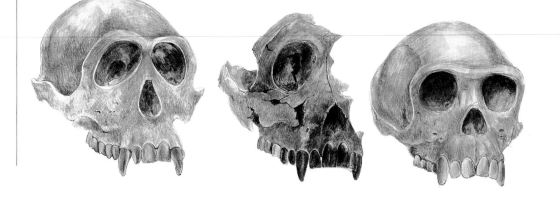

Africa drifted into Eurasia. The Asian branch changed very little, eventually giving rise to the orang-utans which are isolated today in the islands of Borneo and Sumatra.

Evidence from scientists exploring the molecular-clock approach to evolution confirms that *Sivapithecus* could have been the ancestor of orang-utans. The molecular-clock approach involves measuring the genetic differences between two different though related species and using them as a possible yardstick to measure the time that has elapsed since they diverged from a common ancestor. Using this technique, experts discovered that the European and Asian *Sivapithecus* finds were consistent with the view that the orang-utans broke away from the main ape-human line about 10 million years ago. The last remains of orang-utans on the mainland appear to be 23 000-year-old burned and broken bones from a cave in Vietnam, where the creatures were butchered by a Stone Age people.

THE OTHER GORILLAS

The first trace of another candidate for our common ancestor was found in 1856 by a French lawyer and part-time enthusiast for fossil hunting, Edouard Lartet. On a trip to the French Pyrenees, he unearthed an early primate jaw from clay at Saint-Gaudens in the range's foothills. He named the specimen *Dryopithecus*, meaning 'oak ape', because oak leaves had been found alongside the fossils.

Since then evidence has been found of a species of hardy, primitive ape, *Dryopithecus branchoi*, living around 10 million years ago in the wooded swamplands that today are rural Hungary. Its fossilised bones have been found in a giant iron-ore mining pit near the town of Rudabanya, although it is thought to have lived throughout western and southern Europe between 11 and 9 million years ago. It bore some resemblance to a modern gorilla, and is thought to be close to the common ancestor of gorillas, chimps and humans. It does, however, possess features which suggest that gorillas and humans are more distantly related than humans and chimpanzees are.

Before the 1960s, it was argued that there are fundamental differences between all living species of great apes – gorillas, chimpanzees, orang-utans and gibbons – but that they were all members of the same family. Humans, on the other hand, were placed in our own distinct family, the Hominidae. That was before American scientists examined the blood proteins of the great apes and came to the conclusion that gorillas and chimpanzees are more closely related to humans than they are to orang-utans and gibbons. Humans, in

---

GOLDEN AGE OF APES

About 18 million years ago continental drift made Africa, the Arabian Peninsula and Eurasia rejoin. Before this Africa and Eurasia had been separated by a narrow band of sea. The earth movements bringing the continents together were, however, violent, throwing up, for example, the Alps in Europe. The disruption of the circulation of the seas and winds resulted in climate changes and the monkeys and apes took advantage of them. There followed a rich exchange of animals. Monkeys and apes moved into Eurasia. Apes became a very diverse group – but their dispersion was short-lived. By the late Miocene drier savannah conditions started to prevail across what had been woodland belts, restricting the apes to the remaining forest areas.

---

a controversial taxonomic reshuffle, had lost their exclusivity.

Those scientists who studied bones, however, were not convinced. Traditionally, palaeoanthropologists have placed the chimpanzees and the gorillas together. They are, after all, the only animals that walk on their knuckles. Early human ancestors show no signs of having adopted this method of locomotion; therefore chimpanzees and gorillas must have inherited knuckle-walking from a different common ancestor from man. The molecular biologists, however, disagreed. By studying blood proteins and the DNA in the cells of modern chimpanzees and gorillas, they concluded that chimpanzees are mankind's nearest ape relatives, and that gorillas are on a separate evolutionary branch.

YEARS APART *An orang-utan and its human guardian at a Sumatra rehabilitation centre show how apes and people have diverged over 15 million years.*

The evidence from both camps was fairly evenly balanced – that is, until the Hungarian *Dryopithecus* came along. The fossils of this gorilla lookalike showed certain primitive features, such as the shape and setting of the teeth at the front of the mouth, which are absent in modern chimpanzees and humans, but present in modern gorillas. The conclusion was that these features, present in the common ancestor, were lost when chimpanzees and humans split off and evolved separately from the gorillas. As the fossil evidence for the period between 10 and 4 million years ago is fairly sparse, it is possible that the bones of an ape-like hominid will be found which demonstrates that early ancestors on the evolutionary route to man did engage in knuckle-walking.

FOUND IN MACEDONIA

There is more agreement among experts about the Hungarian ape's status as a close relative of the common ancestor of the African apes and humans. There is yet another candidate, however. In Macedonia, a 10-million-year-old fossil with affinities to apes and man was found in September 1989.

The creature has been named *Ouranopithecus macedoniensis* (or in some accounts *Graecopithecus freybergi*). It is represented by a large portion of a male face and several sets of jaws. It, too, has features that link it to gorillas, chimpanzees and early man, especially gorillas. Like *Dryopithecus*, this Greek ape has a downward bending of the face on the brain case, an anatomical change known as klinorhynchy, which is characteristic of the human face and the faces of the African great apes. *Ouranopithecus*, however, shows a greater degree of this change in the shape and position of the face than *Dryopithecus*.

The two European apes also have similar teeth in the upper jaw. The crowns of the incisors are vertical, for example, and the

A GIANT AMONGST APES

One of the relatives of mankind's early ape-like ancestors was a giant. It was a gigantic, gorilla-sized ape with the appropriate scientific name of *Gigantopithecus*. It may have stood some 9 ft (2.7 m) tall and weighed about 600 lb (270 kg), and was the largest known primate ever to have lived.

Its existence first came to light in 1931 when its gigantic teeth were found in traditional pharmacies in Hong Kong where they were labelled dragon's teeth. They were ground down and sold as medicines. The fossilised remains, however, are not native to the island but are to be found in cave deposits in mainland China, India and northern Vietnam. The oldest may date from 8 million years ago and the youngest from less than 1 million.

At first, *Gigantopithecus* was held up as one of man's predecessors. Its canines and incisors were small, like those of later hominids, but its jaws and back teeth were massive, larger than those of a modern gorilla. Evidence suggests that this enormous ape was a shy forest-dweller, living alongside giant pandas, porcupines, tapirs and ancient orang-utans in the dense forests of Asia.

Fossils from China that are as little as half-a-million years old mean that *Gigantopithecus* was living at the same time as modern man. Could those early representatives of mankind have

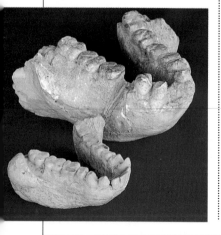

'JAWS' *The lower jaw of ancient* Gigantopithecus *is enormous compared to that of a modern ape. Right: Tibetan refugees fleeing into Nepal are attacked by a* Gigantopithecus-*like yeti. Could the ancient ape still be alive?*

eliminated these giant apes, or did the giant ape survive? Does the legend of the Yeti or abominable snowman indicate that *Gigantopithecus* is alive and well and living in the mountains?

canines are in line with the teeth behind. Such features suggest that both creatures were close to the common ancestor of the African apes and humans. *Ouranopithecus*, however, bears a greater resemblance to the modern gorilla in such features as the size and shape of its brow ridge and the angular shape of the muzzle. The resemblance is so marked that scientists studying the fossils have labelled *Ouranopithecus* a 'second gorilla'.

APES ACROSS AFRICA

While the European fossils of *Dryopithecus branchoi* were being assessed during 1992, a band of French and American fossil hunters chanced upon the fossil jawbone of a long extinct ape in an old mine in Namibia.

They had travelled the dusty 300 miles (480 km) from Windhoek to the Berg Aukas vanadium mine, and were looking forward to a shower, beer and barbecue. They could not resist, however, a first look at the mine and took advantage of the last half-hour or so of daylight. One of the team, scrambling across the debris of rock left over from the mining operations, suddenly muttered the words 'Hullo, here's a jaw' and in a few seconds introduced a new twist to the

KNUCKLE-WALKER *Modern apes, such as chimpanzees, walk on the knuckles of their hands and are reluctant to get wet.*

palaeoanthropologists' understanding of the story of mankind.

Until that moment all the Miocene fossil apes had been found to the north of the Equator, but this discovery opened up the story considerably. Here was evidence that early apes were living to the south of the southerly limit of today's great apes.

The jawbone was assigned to a new species, *Otavipithecus namibiensis* – in honour of the Otavi Mountains where the fossil was found. It had molar teeth with thin enamel, but little wear, indicating that it was probably a soft-fruit eater, like *Proconsul*. It lived about 13 million years ago, 3 million years before the European apes. The date was determined when the cave breccia – rock composed of small fragments cemented together – in which the jawbone was embedded was analysed microscopically. Littered amongst

the grains of sand and fragments of rock were the tiny teeth of bats, shrews, elephant shrews and six species of extinct rodents. They were known to have lived in the middle Miocene, about 13 million years ago. This made the Namibian fossil contemporary with another ancient proto-ape, *Kenyapithecus*, one of the sivapithecines.

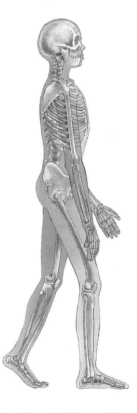

GOING STRAIGHT *Unique adaptations have taken place in the human skeleton to allow us to balance and walk upright on two legs.*

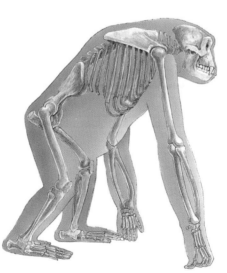

PROCONSUL *This early ape moved on all fours. Its arms were slightly longer than its legs to enable it to balance as it walked along branches.*

GORILLA *The gorilla moves in a semi-upright position, with a sloping back and bent legs. It uses its long arms for support and leans on its knuckles.*

HOMO SAPIENS *Humans have a short pelvis to facilitate walking and an S-shaped spine to support the body in an upright position over long, straight legs.*

In attempting to summarise events in the middle and late Miocene, nobody can paint a clear picture of mankind's development during those critical years. What is certain is that the lines which would later give rise to the higher primates of today began to diverge. There are also some general trends. The first group to diverge was the lesser apes, the gibbons and siamangs, followed by the line which gave rise to the orang-utans. Later still, the remaining hominid stock branched again, leading to the gorillas, chimpanzees, bonobos (pygmy chimpanzees) and humans.

The detail of that divergence is still denied to scientists. There are simply too few fossils available. The period is known to those who study the origins of mankind as 'the hominid gap', and whatever happened in the gap was far more complicated than was once imagined, with many species of primeval apes evolving simultaneously.

ANCESTRAL HOME *The common ancestor of the higher primates probably lived in the wooded savannah of tropical Africa. Below: The 10-million-year-old skull of an adult male Ouranopithecus was found in Macedonia.*

THE TIME OF LUCY

The habit of walking upright is one of the hallmarks of the hominids – the forebears of modern man. A creature living in Ethiopia more than 4 million years ago may have walked upright; 'Lucy', living 3 million years ago, definitely did.

The earliest member of the human family we know of emerged around 4.4 million years ago. Its remains were found in northeastern Ethiopia in 1994 by a team of palaeontologists from the Universities of Tokyo and California at Berkeley. The fossil site was in Ethiopia's Afar Depression, at a hot and barren place to the west of the Awash river in 'badlands' – an area of eroded peaks, ridges and plateaus – near the village of Aramis.

Today, temperatures at Aramis can reach 50°C (120°F) in the shade . . . except that there is little shade for there are few trees. Four million years ago, by contrast, the place was a flat plain covered with woods and forests. Colobus monkeys and other tree-dwelling creatures climbed in the trees, while kudu antelopes roamed the forest floor. Alongside them was a very special ape-like creature, a hominid – a member of the family that would later produce *Homo sapiens*, modern man. It climbed about in the canopy in search of fruit, and made forays on to the ground to forage and to cross from one stand of trees to the next. It may have stood upright to reach for fruit in trees. Whether or not it walked on two legs is uncertain, although some of the fossil bones discovered at Aramis suggest that it might have done.

BETWEEN APES AND MEN

Pieces of skull, numerous teeth and broken arm bones from 16 adults were found, together with a child's lower jawbone complete with milk tooth. The opening at the base of one skull fragment – the *foramen magnum* through which the spinal cord connects to the brain – is seen to be farther forward than in other apes, suggesting that the head was balanced on top of an upright backbone.

From the cranium fragments found, it is thought that the brain was relatively small – smaller than that of a chimpanzee (modern man's closest relative among the apes). The small size of its teeth and the thin enamel were similar to those in the chimpanzee, suggesting a diet of soft fruit and berries – creatures eating tougher foods, such as leaves, develop thicker enamel. The canine teeth were more like those of a human: they were blunt and diamond-shaped, whereas ape teeth are pointed and V-shaped. Taken together these different features pointed to an ape-like creature intermediate between chimps and the line that led to humans.

In due course, scientists gave this ancient hominid the name of *Ardipithecus ramidus*. Discovering it narrowed considerably the gap stretching between the earliest-known hominids and the even earlier common ancestor of the apes and humans, which, according to the molecular-clock approach (using genetic evidence to work out when particular evolutionary lines started to diverge) should have lived between 6 and 4 million years ago.

The discovery of the fossil bones in beds which contain evidence of forests, and the hint that the creature might have walked around on two legs, rather than on all fours, was important. They suggest that, contrary to what many experts had previously thought, the spreading of savannah across Africa was not necessarily the main stimulus

FIRST BIPED *The lightly built* **Australopithecus afarensis** *walked upright, but also had the long arms and curled fingers of a tree-climber.*

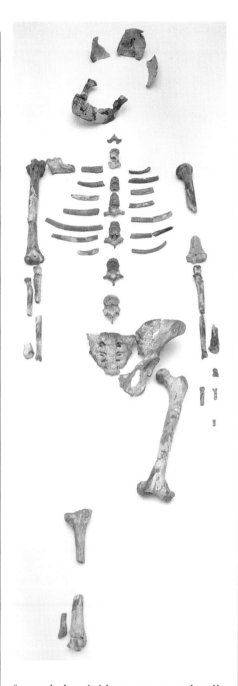

LUCY FROM ETHIOPIA *About 40 per cent of the skeleton of a 20-year-old female* A. afarensis *shows adaptations to upright walking. Right: A gorilla's long, curled fingers allow it to grip branches when climbing and to hold objects firmly.*

fect on our understanding of our distant ancestors and how they evolved. Around 47 miles (75 km) north-east of Aramis is Hadar, a remote place now, which none the less represents an important milestone in human evolution. It was here, at Afar Locality 288 (in scientific jargon), in rocks dated to 3.5 million years ago, that a primate was discovered in 1974 that stood, walked and ran on two legs.

LUCY OF ETHIOPIA

The skeleton, which was of an adult female, seemed in many ways to be remarkably like our own. The scientists who discovered her gave her the nickname 'Lucy', after the Beatles' song 'Lucy in the Sky with Diamonds'. She is also sometimes known by her Ethiopian name of Danikenesh which means 'you are wonderful', and wonderful she turned out to be.

Lucy was given the official scientific name *Australopithecus afarensis: Australopithecus*, meaning 'southern ape', and *afarensis*, 'of the Afar'. About 40 per cent of her skeleton was discovered, making her the most complete fossilised skeleton from these ancient times. She stood just 3 ft 8 in (1.1 m) tall, although others of her kind – especially the males who were noticeably bigger than the females – may have grown much taller, to a height of 5 ft 6 in (1.7 m). She weighed about 65 lb (30 kg).

She had strong muscles and dense limb bones, evidence that she walked upright. She had an ape-like face and large, jutting jaws. Her brain was about a quarter the size of a modern human's, no bigger than a chimpanzee's. The skull was long and low, with a pronounced crest at the back of the head, to which large neck muscles were attached to steady the head.

The way her teeth were formed lay some-

where between those of humans and chimpanzees – the canines were large but reduced, with male canines larger than those of the female. The arms were long as with other early hominids. The hands were curved, indicating a link with a tree-dwelling lifestyle, and they had attachments for powerful wrists as in apes – these help the apes to swing through the trees. The thumb was

---

LUCY'S BABY

Birth was slow and difficult for Lucy's children. Examination of her pelvic bones shows that the birth canal was widest from side to side, flared at the top and narrow at the bottom. Lucy's children had small brains, so a broad canal was unnecessary. The modern human birth canal is wide at the top, but becomes less wide halfway down and deeper from front to back. Thus a baby faces the side until midway when it must rotate its head. The australopithecine baby entered the canal with the head facing the side and left it like that, probably with the head tilted slightly to ease its passage through the narrow pelvic outlet.

---

shorter than the modern human thumb, and the fingers, unlike modern human fingers, had narrow rather than square tips – this made them more like a chimpanzee's fingers. By comparing Lucy's hands with

for early hominids to get up and walk. Other factors experts have suggested include the growing weight of the earliest hominids which made tree-living more precarious. Then, once on the ground and walking upright, the creatures would have discovered some of the advantages this way of life brought them – such as the ability to carry loads.

Less than a million years later another hominid appeared on the Earth, and finding its fossil remains was to have a crucial ef-

WALKING UPRIGHT

BIPEDAL WALKER *Sifakas, like all lemurs, can walk on two legs as ancient hominids might have done.*

are spaced well apart. Poor thigh muscles mean that the chimp's body collapses towards the unsupported side. The chimp must therefore shift its centre of gravity to bring its weight in line with the weight-bearing leg at every step. Powerful thigh muscles in humans keep us upright.

Humans did not get where they are today by a direct change from walking on all fours to walking upright. Instead, an evolutionary trend throughout primate history has led to upright walking. Our first prosimian ancestors had the habit of erect clinging and leaping, as their descendants the lemurs, tarsiers and lorises do today. Monkeys and apes walked on all fours but sat upright, while some apes, such as gibbons and orang-utans, moved through the trees hanging from the undersides of branches.

Why humans decided to walk at all is the subject of controversy. In the 1960s, the anthropological world offered 'man the hunter' as an explanation. Early humans, it was said, were able to track prey much more efficiently than a quadruped; they had more stamina, although they were less proficient in the chase.

Then came the 'man the scavenger' hypothesis. Humans would have been able to follow herds and scavenge the carcasses of the old, infirm and unfortunate newborn. By standing on two legs our ancestors also had early warning of distant predators.

The overwhelming evidence from fossil teeth, however, is that early hominids ate mainly plants not meat. Therefore, in the 1970s, the switch to 'woman the gatherer' and more recently 'man the provisioner' were proposed. There was a need to carry things. The 'gatherer' hypothesis envisaged women travelling long distances to forage for themselves and their infants. They carried the food and their offspring with them, hence the need to walk upright on two legs. The 'provisioner' hypothesis sees male hominids gathering the food and bringing it back to a home-base where it was shared with the females and infants.

A more recent hypothesis suggests that the ability to walk upright was simply a response to changes in the distribution of food resources. On a more open savannah, food would become thinly dispersed and upright walking was the most efficient way to travel. Our ancient ancestors took advantage of this improved method of locomotion. It was their way of surviving where other apes could not.

Lucy's long leg bones demonstrate that she was well adapted to upright walking. Other related adaptations were her flaring pelvis which carried gluteal muscles to the side of the thigh for stability, the angle of her femur which brought her weight under her body and the human-like knee, with a large flat surface at the bottom of the femur, which transmitted weight through the extended leg. All these, together with the arched foot which served as a shock absorber, permitted her body weight to be moved forward smoothly and with little muscle fatigue.

Humans are not alone in being able to walk upright; on occasions chimpanzees and gorillas can do it,

too. The chimpanzee's gait, however, is quite erratic. It sways from side to side at every step. Unlike humans and Lucy, the centre of gravity – higher in chimps than in humans – must shift towards the leg on the ground while the other leg swings. In humans the sloping angle of the thigh bone, from the thigh to the knee – the valgus angle – brings the feet under the mid-line of the body, and so the body need not sway. In chimps the angle is not so pronounced and so the feet

LEGGING IT *Compared to the gorilla, the human leg and its muscles are structured so that the leg can be straightened and extended for upright walking.*

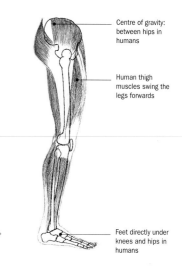

Centre of gravity: in front of hips in gorillas

Gorilla's thigh muscles swing the legs sideways

Feet at angle from knees in gorillas

Centre of gravity: between hips in humans

Human thigh muscles swing the legs forwards

Feet directly under knees and hips in humans

those of modern humans and other primates, experts have established that she had sufficient manipulative ability to throw small round objects – though they have no evidence that she actually did.

It is thought that Lucy had a bent-hip, bent-knee form of walking like a modern chimpanzee and her general shape was probably more like a short, squat ape than a slim, upright human.

More recently, in 1994, an Israeli scientist from Tel Aviv University, working in the Hadar region, practically stubbed his toe on the one piece of evidence of *Australo-pithecus afarensis* that was missing from the fossil record – a complete skull. Identified by its catalogue name of #444, the skull confirmed what had already been deduced from the fragments of Lucy's skull. In brain size and the shape of the skull, this was definitely a creature on the way from being an ape to being a human.

FEET ON THE GROUND

In Pliocene times, about 5 to 2 million years ago, geological changes in Europe, Asia and Africa, resulting in the formation of new mountain ranges, caused regional alterations in climate and vegetation. In East Africa the forests of wetter and warmer times receded and were replaced by a seasonal flora of woodland, wooded grassland, scrub and grassland. It was cooler, drier and there were distinct wet and dry seasons. Lucy therefore lived in a landscape that was less forested than it had been for her ancestors. Her homes were on the lightly wooded lake shores of Hadar and the by now relatively dry and open uplands of East Africa.

Mobile ankle joints and curved fingers enabled her and her friends to climb trees, just as children do today, but the greater part of their life was probably spent with their feet planted firmly on the ground. These hominids had to be nimble movers, just like the pigs, cattle and antelope which shared the grasslands. They had to follow the rains just as savannah animals do today.

At Hadar, there was a freshwater lake, with numerous rivers and streams running into it from the Ethiopian Plateau. Fossil tur-

EAST AFRICAN HOME *Open woodland around the Masai Mara river is the type of habitat that Lucy and her kind would have lived in.*

FOLLOWING IN LUCY'S FOOTSTEPS

Fossilised footprints made in soft, damp volcanic ash about 3.7 million years ago at Laetoli in Tanzania show the toe and arch of early bipeds, probably *Australopithecus afarensis* – relatives of Lucy. The prints show that one of our earliest special characteristics was not a large brain, language or toolmaking – none of which were characteristics of Lucy and her kind – but the ability to walk upright.

The footprints were a remarkable discovery for ichnologists (scientists who study fossil footprints). The first ones were discovered by people working with Mary Leakey in 1978. They showed a squarish heel and the bones were arranged almost exactly like those in a modern human foot. Indeed, if the footprints were not known to be so old, scientists would probably have thought they were made by members of our own species walking barefoot.

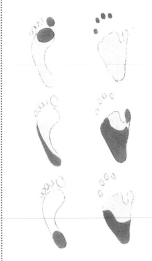

VITAL CLUE *Footprints at Laetoli show the same pattern of weight distribution as in modern humans, proving that A. afarensis walked upright.*

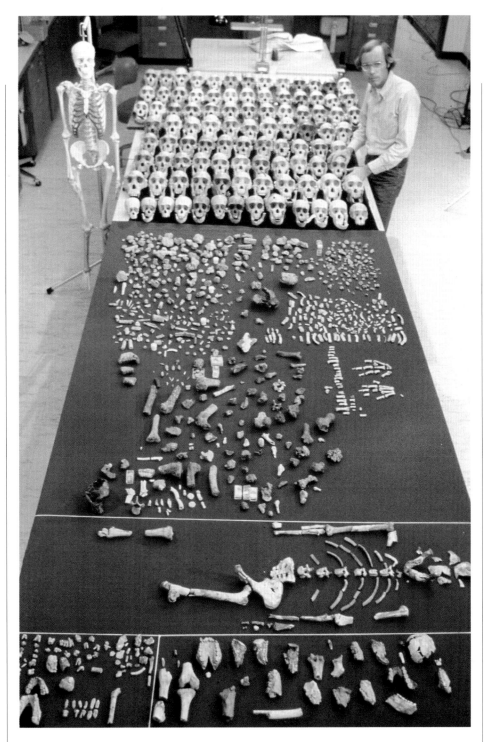

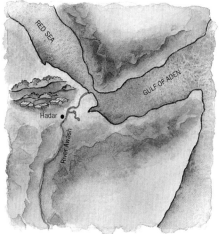

HEIRLOOMS *Excavations at Hadar in Ethiopia have yielded numerous hominid remains (above), including fragments of an A. afarensis skeleton (left, near the front of the table).*

By 2.5 million years ago grassland and heath were replacing the montane forests.

Lucy and her family probably gathered fruit and foliage from the trees. They may also have slept in them as chimpanzees do today, building night nests, perhaps for comfort and to put them safely out of the reach of the predators that roamed the savannah at night. A robust upper right-arm bone, found in 1990, indicates that powerful shoulder muscles would have been able to hoist Lucy's body up into the trees using her arms. As for food, Lucy of necessity had a catholic diet. She was an opportunist, travelling long distances between clumped, seasonal sources of water and food, particularly plant food.

Lucy and her kind were not confined to the Hadar lakeshore, for the fossilised remains of 80 or more other individuals attributed to the same species have been found in Ethiopia and Tanzania in rocks dated between 3.9 and 3 million years ago. In northern Kenya, a specimen has been tentatively dated to 5.6 million years old. If this dating is correct, it would make the creature the oldest-known australopithecine and the closest one to the date of the divergence of man-like hominids from the apes.

tle and crocodile eggs and a preserved crab's claw indicate not only the presence of water 3 million years ago but also possible high-protein food for the hominids. The lake fluctuated in level during the time Lucy, her predecessors and descendants were alive. The sediments and gravels rapidly buried the creatures that died on the shore, turning them into fossils which would tantalise scientists hundreds of millennia later.

Stretches of forest probably lined the river banks, just as trees line the Mara river in East Africa today, and thick woods most likely fringed the lake. The forests were not extensive, however, for fossil evidence suggests that the savannah came close to the lake shore. Away from the lakeside the land was covered with grass and scattered stands of trees. The nearest tropical forest to survive the change in climate was probably on the mountains on either side of the Great Rift. But even here the vegetation was changing.

THE SOUTHERN APE-MAN

The australopithecines – southern ape-men – flourished from about 3 million years ago in eastern and southern Africa. Upright walkers, with increasing brain sizes, they were the immediate ancestors of the earliest species of Homo.

Professor Raymond Dart of Witwatersrand University in South Africa was just leaving home one day in 1924 to go to a friend's wedding when miners from a lime quarry brought him two boxes of rock. Contained in one of them was an 'endocranial cast', the nearest thing to a fossilised brain – in fact, the fossilised cast of the inside of a skull. This cast came from the skull of a man-like ape that died more than 2 million years ago, becoming entombed in the Taung cave near Kimberley.

The wedding over, Dart returned to his fossils. Looking carefully at the shiny, brown cast, he was able to see the tracks of fissures and blood vessels that would have been on the surface of the brain. A search of the boxes revealed parts of the skull, including the forehead and face. It had no brow ridges, and the jaw did not protrude like that of an ape. Milk teeth, and emerging first molars, revealed that the skull was a child's. The way in which the skull would have balanced on the spinal column indicated that the child stood upright, leaving its hands free. When grown up, suggested Dart, it could have used weapons and tools.

By counting the incremental growth lines on the teeth as well as examining the way in which the teeth erupted, scientists have now estimated that the Taung youngster must have been about three years old when it died. But it was the size of a six-year-old human equivalent. The man-apes evidently had offspring that developed rapidly like young apes, rather than slowly like human children.

SOUTHERNER **Australopithecus africanus** *was fully adapted to an upright life. It could handle objects but there is no evidence that it used tools.*

Dart himself was 32 years old at the time of the discovery, and he was well aware of its historic importance. He wrote that it represented 'the penultimate phase in human evolution'. The world's press had a 'missing link' field day, but Dart's peers in the scientific community were less impressed. Large-brained fossils were emerging from the Far East and so researchers felt that Africa was not the place to find the progenitors of modern man. There was also the infamous, large-brained, ape-jawed 'Piltdown Man', which was dominating anthropological debate. It turned out to be a hoax, but at the time it was taken seriously by the academics.

Dart's new discovery did not fit in with current thinking. He was ridiculed by the elite members of the scientific 'establishment' who wanted to see their own, and as it turned out rather shaky, theories as correct. He stepped back from the controversy and concentrated on medical science.

FINDING THE SOUTHERN APE-MEN

Robert Broom, an older palaeontologist from Scotland, took up the challenge. He was an ardent supporter of Dart and said so. 'Here was a man', announced Broom, 'who . . . made one of the greatest discoveries in the world's history and English culture treats him like a naughty schoolboy.' Broom went in search of more fossils.

In May 1936, the Taung child was followed by some bone fragments from adult specimens of the same species found in quarries at Sterkfontein, near Johannesburg. The bones that Broom uncovered pointed to an upright creature which was more hominid than ape. It had a small brain and human-like teeth, the very opposite of the Piltdown forgery. Broom kept digging. By 1948, when he was 81 years old, Broom had uncovered enough evidence to suggest that not one but at least two man-apes, as they became known, existed in southern Africa. One form of man-ape was believed to be more slender and lightly built (it became

SHORT-LIVED MAN-APES

Some studies of teeth suggest that the gracile form, *Australopithecus africanus*, may have had a lifespan of about 22 years on average, whereas *Australopithecus robustus* survived for perhaps just 17 years. This compares with a modern chimpanzee which lives for 40-45 years, the orang-utan with 35 years in the wild, and the lowland gorilla with 35 years – if human poachers do not get to them first, that is.

known as 'gracile'); the other form was more robust. These man-apes followed the two older species *Ardipithecus ramidus*, which was found in rocks dated 4.4 million years ago, and *Australopithecus afarensis* (Lucy), which lived 3.9 to 3 million years ago.

The Taung baby was one of the gracile types, and it was given the scientific name *Australopithecus africanus*, meaning 'southern ape of Africa'. When adult it would have

DART AND FRIEND *South African palaeontologist Professor Raymond Dart with the original Taung fossil of A. africanus.*

been not much bigger than *Australopithecus afarensis*, but with a slightly larger brain, larger back teeth and smaller front ones. It lived from about 3 to 2.5 million years ago.

The other, robust form was called *Australopithecus robustus* or *Paranthropus* ('near man') *robustus*. It lived later than *africanus*, between about 1.9 and 1.6 million years ago, and it was an altogether more powerful creature than Dart's Taung child. It had a face with no forehead and flared cheek bones which provided an anchor for chewing muscles. These features combined to give the face a sunken 'dish' shape. It had a pronounced crest running along the top of the skull, like that of a gorilla, to which a second set of powerful chewing muscles was attached to work the lower jaw.

The incisors and canines were small and blade-like, and the teeth rows were tucked under the face rather than protruding, which helped in chewing. It had large, flat grinding back teeth. This robust ape-man was the ultimate chewing machine, designed to deal with nuts, hard-shelled fruits and fibrous roots. Unlike the gracile forms, which would have stayed close to the remaining woodlands of their time, it lived in more open, drier conditions. It would have encountered fewer soft fruits, probably a staple food of the gracile forms, depending more on

TAUNG BABY *The shape and angle of the skull and the design of the jaws convinced Professor Dart that his find was more human than ape.*

tough seeds designed to withstand times of drought.

In the South American rain forest a pair of New World monkeys provide modern parallels with the gracile and robust life styles. Neither exists in the kind of arid conditions in which the man-apes lived, but they do show jaw and teeth adaptations to different kinds of fruit. One is the slender spider monkey which has normal monkey-like teeth and eats only ripe fleshy fruits. The other is its neighbour, the bearded saki. This more robust monkey feeds on unripe seeds and those encased in a tough coat. It not only possesses extremely strong teeth but also the incisors project forwards, with the upper set positioned to overbite the lower ones, much like a parrot's beak. With this arrangement the bearded saki can deal with the toughest husks and the hardest nuts, such as Brazil nuts.

NUTCRACKER MAN

Later finds from East Africa and Ethiopia revealed that there was a diverse group of man-apes living during this explosive period in the story of mankind. An even more powerful robust form, for example, was discovered in East Africa. It had a more massive head and teeth than *robustus* and

HUNTER OR HUNTED?

The robust australopithecines were large animals, similar in stature to gorillas. But they differed from them in one key aspect of life in the wild – in their vulnerability to predators. Modern gorillas are not by and large vulnerable – except when it comes to man the poacher – whereas robust ape-men were. Several skulls of *Australopithecus robustus*, found in cave excavations at Swartkrans, South Africa, are perforated. The holes, about $^1/4$ in (6 mm) across, are found in pairs, each hole 1 $^1/4$ in (32 mm) from its partner. At first, blows from a pointed weapon were offered as explanation, but more recently parallels have been drawn between these wounds and the puncture marks made by the teeth of leopards in the skulls of baboons.

Early man-apes could have driven off the carnivores by screaming, throwing sticks and stones, and charging, just as baboons and chimpanzees do today, but at night while sleeping, they were vulnerable.

Baboons regularly fall prey to leopards. The leopards seek out the monkeys' sleeping sites and ambush them at night. Leopards, so the evidence suggests, adopted a similar hunting strategy more than a million years ago when they crept up on robust man-apes in their caves. The absence of *Homo* skulls from such caves suggests that the ancestors of our own species did not fall for the leopard's predatory trick.

HOMINIDS AS PREY *Asleep in a cave, a hominid was easy prey. Right: The puncture marks in an ape-man skull match the position of the large canine teeth in a leopard's jaw.*

so was nicknamed 'Nutcracker Man'. It was discovered in 1959 by Mary Leakey, when it was known as *Zinjanthropus* ('East African Man') *boisei* or 'Zinj'. It was unleashed on the anthropological world exactly 100 years after Darwin had published his *On the Origin of Species*. Coinciding with this centenary, it received considerable publicity, fuelling another round of press speculation about the 'missing link'. It was not the missing link, however, and was later re-assigned to the species *Australopithecus* or *Paranthropus boisei*, an evolutionary dead-end. It lived between 2.1 and 1.5 million years ago.

It is not certain if all the species of australopithecines have been found because new fossils are being unearthed almost daily. Where these different species, with their varying degrees of robustness, overlapped in time, they might well have occupied completely different habitats, in the way that chimpanzees and gorillas do today. Or each species might have lived side by side, sharing the same habitat like Old World monkeys today.

In the Kibale Forest of western Uganda, for example, two distinct species of colobus monkeys co-exist in the same patch of forest because of a subtle difference in their feeding habits. Red colobus monkeys have to range over a large area, up to 86 acres (35 ha), in order to find young leaves on which they feed exclusively, while black-and-white colobus monkeys, which also favour young leaves, will resort to tougher, mature leaves if circumstances force them to do so. Surrounded by an assured food supply they have a home range half that of the red colobus monkeys. The two species live in relative harmony just as some of the australopithecines might have done.

THE ART OF WALKING UPRIGHT

All the forms that have so far been discovered shared an important feature: they were all bipedal – that is, they walked upright. The shape of the thigh bone, where it articulated with the pelvis, however, was more

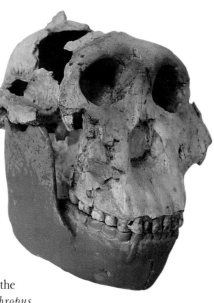

NUTCRACKER MAN *The 'Zinjanthropus' skull from Olduvai Gorge, Tanzania, was later labelled* A. boisei, *and proved an evolutionary dead-end. Right: A drawing of* A. boisei *based on the skull.*

primitive than it is in modern humans. The australopithecine thigh bone or femur had a smaller head where it joined the pelvis, and a thinner neck than in later hominids, which suggests that these creatures moved with a slightly different gait than that of modern man.

The hands of later australopithecines were more advanced than those of, say, Lucy. The thumb was long and mobile, and the fingertips were wide, an indication than they had a good blood supply and were well served with nerve endings, giving them a greater sensitivity to touch. It is quite possible that these southern man-apes were capable of shaping and using simple stone tools.

The males were considerably taller and heavier than the females, unlike male and female chimpanzees and humans where the difference in size is less noticeable. They roamed their scrub and savannah woodland home in groups in much the same way that bands of chimpanzees do today. They shared their living space with troops of baboons with which they must have competed and sometimes clashed.

Teeth and jaws were adapted to grinding food, which was probably mainly vegetarian. At one time the lighter eating apparatus of the ancient gracile man-apes was thought to indicate that they were meat-eaters, but more recent analysis of tooth wear suggests a fruit-eating diet similar to that of chimpanzees and orang-utans. Modern chimps, however, are partial to flesh, and there is some evidence that both forms of the australopithecines took advantage of meat when it was available. They might have scavenged on carnivore kills, eating meat and bone marrow from the limbs of antelopes

MIGHTY CHEWERS, DELICATE ANIMALS

The terms gracile and robust used to refer to the bodily build of the australopithecines. But their fossil bones have been re-examined by scientists at Tel Aviv University who came to the conclusion that the difference between them was more in the teeth, jaws and parts of the face and head where the muscles for chewing are attached. The robust forms were not, in fact, heavily built individuals, as was

continued on page 40

OLDUVAI GORGE

ouis and Mary Leakey first visited Olduvai Gorge in Tanzania in 1931. They soon realised they had chanced on a treasure house of anthropological finds, for the gorge contains remains and artefacts from 2 million to just 10 000 years ago.

The gorge is a 25 mile (40 km) long, 330 ft (100 m) deep river-carved canyon dissecting an ancient lake basin on the Serengeti Plain. The fossils are found in rocks which are arranged like a layer cake and can be dated with reasonable accuracy. In some places, the gorge cuts through hominid camp sites and butchering sites. Some of the oldest stone tools, crudely flaked pebbles, were found here. Whether these were fashioned by australopithecines or by the evolving *Homo* species, the remains of which are also found in the gorge, is still unclear.

Many significant fossils have been found including the skull of *Zinjanthropus* (*Australopithecus boisei*) in 1959. The discovery was made by Mary Leakey, quite by accident. Louis was in bed with flu and Mary went for a walk with the dogs when she spotted a fragment of bone. Brushing aside the soil she revealed hominid teeth, and when the fossil was fully excavated the Leakeys found themselves holding the complete undamaged skull of a robust australopithecine.

FOSSIL-RICH GORGE *Remains of* Australopithecus boisei, Homo habilis *and* Homo erectus *have all been found in different parts of Olduvai Gorge.*

Australopithecus boisei

Homo habilis

Homo erectus

once thought. Their massive chewing system was imposed on a relatively lightly built animal. The cranium or brain case, for example, was very thin, no more than $^4/_{25}$ in (4 mm) thick in the larger specimens.

Although skull sizes can be measured with some degree of accuracy, brain sizes are more difficult to assess. Fossil skulls are often filled with fine-grained rock which is difficult to remove without destroying the specimen. However, employing the computer-controlled X-ray machines more usually used to scan patients with brain tumours, researchers at the Washington University Medical School in St Louis, Missouri, examined the skulls of gracile man-apes. Taking 50 X-ray slices through a skull, they constructed a three-dimensional image of the inner brain case. The researchers made two significant discoveries. The brain volume was 10 per cent less than had been previously thought – 27 cu in (442 cm³) on average, the size of a chimpanzee's brain.

This pointed to the second finding: that man evolved feet first, rather than brain first – our brains grew larger a long time after we walked upright.

THE BLACK SKULL

In 1985, the cranium of a robust australopithecine, known as the 'black skull', was discovered on the west side of Lake Turkana in northern Kenya. Its dark colour came from staining by manganese minerals. It was found to be about 2.5 million years old, and it was an unusual find. It had a large, curved face like the face of a robust australopithecine, but the top and back of the small brain case were more like that of Lucy. It had a forward-jutting, ape-like lower face, an extremely large palate and large tooth sockets.

The date of this skull was important. Because the gracile australopithecines lived before the robust ones that had so far been discovered, it was assumed that they were on or close to the evolutionary line leading to the robust forms. Here, however, was a robust form living at the same time as the gracile species. The likeliest explanation was that it evolved from a Lucy-like *Australopithecus afarensis* and could have been evolving into a robust *Australopithecus boisei*. It has been given the name *Australopithecus aethiopicus*.

THE FAMILY BUSH

Clearly the age of the australopithecines was important in the story of man, for at some time during this period an upright, large-brained creature emerged that was to be our first human-like ancestor, founder of the genus *Homo*. From the number

ANCIENT JAWS *A large number of australopithecine jaws were found at the Hadar sites in Ethiopia in deposits dating back 2.6 to 3.3 million years.*

BLACK SKULL *The manganese-stained skull is that of a robust ape-man,* A. aethiopicus, *from Kenya, which evolved from a Lucy-like ancestor.*

of man-ape species available and the speed with which anatomical changes were taking place, the evolutionary tree has turned into something more like a bush. From the many hypotheses put forward over the years, two have stood the test of time.

The first hypothesis holds that *Australopithecus afarensis* (Lucy) was close to the common ancestor of all later hominids. It led in one direction to *Australopithecus aethiopicus*, and was related to, if not the ancestor of, the robust australopithecines. In the other direction it led to *Australopithecus africanus* and the genus *Homo*.

The second hypothesis proposes that *Australopithecus afarensis* gave rise in one direction to *Australipithecus boisei* (including *Australopithecus aethiopicus*, which some consider the same species), and in the other direction to *Australopithecus africanus*, which gave rise to *Australopithecus robustus*. The *Homo* lineage is said, by the proponents of this notion, to be too obscure to determine.

Whatever the view, the role played by *Australopithecus africanus*, the species discovered by Dart, is, as one researcher put it, still 'pivotal after more than 60 years of controversy'.

PILTDOWN MAN: THE SUPREME PRACTICAL JOKE

At the time the australopithecines were being found in southern Africa, an extraordinary story was unfolding in England. Between 1908 and 1916, fossils from a gravel pit near the village of Piltdown, Sussex, supported a view held by certain palaeoanthropologists that the feature which dominated man's evolution was the enlargement of the brain, not standing upright. The fossils indicated an early man-like creature with a large brain but ape-like jaws. It was given the name *Eoanthropus*, meaning 'dawn man', and it was proof, they thought arrogantly, that Englishmen had taken the lead in evolution, as in so many other things.

The finder was Charles Dawson, a local amateur fossil hunter, and he gave them to Arthur Smith Woodward, the Keeper of Geology at the Natural History Museum in London. The reconstructed skull was presented to the scientific community in 1912, at a pre-Christmas meeting at the Geological Society of London.

Some scientists were highly sceptical and questioned the validity of the find. They pointed out that the reconstructed skull left no space for the windpipe or gullet. Nevertheless, no less an authority than Grafton Elliot Smith, an expert on the brain and evolution, asked the question 'why should nature have played the amazing trick of depositing in the same bed of gravel the brain case, without the jaw, of a hitherto un-known type of early Pleistocene Man displaying unique simian traits, alongside the jaw, without the brain case, of an equally unknown Pleistocene Ape displaying human traits unknown in any Ape?' The argument had no answer, and Piltdown Man was to reign supreme for many years, casting doubt on genuine finds, such as that of Dart in 1924-5, in other parts of the world.

In fact, Piltdown Man was a forgery. Joseph Weiner, a young anatomist from Oxford, with a colleague from Oxford and another from the Natural History Museum, uncovered the scam in the early 1950s. They revealed that the fossil had the jaw of a modern orang-utan attached to the skull of modern man, perhaps from an Egyptian tomb. The teeth were filed down, and the bones stained to look like real fossils. They were placed in the pit along with other fossils and stone tools. There was also the leg bone of an extinct elephant carved to look like a cricket bat – appropriate for the 'first Englishman'. At the time that the 'remains' were discovered, Smith Woodward had asserted of this find in particular that it was 'a supremely important example of the work of palaeolithic man'. The affair was embarrassing for all concerned. Although some scientists had always had doubts, many, notably Smith Woodward, had fallen for the hoax hook, line and sinker.

Who perpetrated it? The answer finally emerged in May 1996 and followed the discovery some years earlier of an old canvas travelling trunk in a loft of the Natural History Museum. It bore the initials of Martin A.C. Hinton, one-time Keeper of Zoology at the museum – a well-known practical joker who stated in his entry in *Who's Who* that he was interested in hoaxes. Inside the trunk were bones that had been stained and carved in exactly the same way as the forged fossils and artefacts at Piltdown. Hinton, it seems, had fallen out with Smith Woodward over a question of research funding. His career had suffered as a result and the hoax was his revenge. How much

PILTDOWN FORGERY *The infamous Piltdown skull that supposedly accommodated the enlarged brain of early man was found in Sussex, England (below). Although it fooled some of the scientific community for several decades, it proved to be a composite of modern orang-utan and human bones.*

Charles Dawson, the 'finder' of the skull, knew about the forgery remains unknown. As an enthusiastic, but not always well-informed, amateur, he was certainly an ideal dupe. For his part, Hinton kept quiet about his role in this supreme practical joke right until his death in 1961.

The entire episode had a profound effect on the story of mankind as it was told for much of the 20th century. The feeling that a large brain preceded upright walking dominated science, and it took many years of painstaking work to reverse that interpretation of events.

THE ARRIVAL OF THE HANDYMAN

Homo habilis – handyman – was the first man-like creature known definitely to have used tools. He also acquired a taste for meat, supplementing his otherwise vegetarian diet with meat scavenged from dead animals.

The small-brained large-jawed australopithecines were not the only hominids living in Africa about 2 million years ago. Alongside them was another group with larger brains and smaller jaws. Whether their brains were large enough to be included rightfully in the genus *Homo*, the genus that contains modern man, is a matter of some controversy, but the general view is that they did belong there.

The average brain size for a modern adult human is just over 82 cu in (1344 cm³), the full range extending from about 61 to 122 cu in (1000 and 2000 cm³). From the late 1940s most experts believed that a fossil skull had to have a brain size of 45³/4 cu in (750 cm³) to be included in the genus *Homo*. That was until 1964, when a group of scientists suggested the 'cerebral rubicon' should be lowered to 36³/5 cu in (600 cm³). What prompted them to make the change was the discovery in the Olduvai Gorge, Tanzania, of hominid fossils they felt were on the direct line to mankind. The estimated brain size of the new discovery was about 41¹/2 cu in (680 cm³).

The fossils belonged to the first truly human-like hominid, a creature given the name *Homo habilis*, the 'handyman', and they were found on the same site and in the same fossil beds as *Zinjanthropus* (*Australopithecus boisei*) or 'Nutcracker Man'.

Homo habilis had a primitive but delicate face and an enlarged brain: about half as large again as *Australopithecus africanus*, though still about half the size of modern human brains. The bones of the cranium are thinner in *Homo* than in *Australopithecus*. More significantly, the brain had the neurological wherewithal for speech – an enlarged Broca's area, the part of the brain associated with speech. *Homo habilis* may therefore have been a speaking animal, though its repertoire of sounds would have been much more limited than ours.

The jaws and teeth are generally smaller and less like a grinding machine than in other hominids, and the tooth rows are tucked under the face. The front teeth, however, are larger. All the teeth have a thick coating of enamel. The pattern of tooth wear suggests a main diet of fruit, very similar to that of the gracile man-apes.

The original collection of *Homo habilis* fossils included hand bones, and it was clear to the scientists who found them that this hominid had the ability to make and use primitive tools. Stone artefacts, including scrapers, choppers and sharp flakes, have been found at *Homo habilis* sites.

SCAVENGING WITH THE FIRST STONE TOOLS

The earliest-known stone tools were found in Ethiopia in deposits about 2.5 million years old. Forty-seven flakes and three large core stones, from which the flakes would have been struck, were made by an unknown hominid, possibly *Homo*. But by far the greatest collection of early stone tools, of a kind that came to be called Oldowan tools, was found at Olduvai Gorge, dated from 2 million years ago and later. The tools and cut-marks on the bones of prey animals suggest that these early hominids were supplementing their fruit diet by eating raw

TOOLMAKER *Homo habilis was a gatherer and scavenger who had the ability to make and use primitive tools such as scrapers and choppers.*

OUT OF KENYA *The skull of* Homo habilis *discovered by Richard Leakey's team in Kenya in 1972 is 1.9 million years old.*

meat and marrow. The fragmented bones of giraffes, hippos and other large game, particularly cattle and antelope, have stone-induced cut-marks which suggest that early humans – a term that can justifiably be used of these creatures – were not only cutting the flesh off the bone, but also cutting away tendons and skin which could be used to bind things together. Meat-eating was not necessarily common. Early humans were opportunists and omnivores – just as modern humans are today.

There were two sources of bodies: big-cat kills, animals killed by, say, a leopard and then cached in a tree, which the hominids raided; and large animals which died of natural causes or drowned. The comparatively puny hominids had to compete for carcasses with the large carnivores of the day – hyenas, lions and sabre-toothed cats. They would have to be quick, too, for hyenas can home in on a corpse long before the vultures have descended.

Meat from these sources would have been important in the dry season, when plant foods – particularly fruits – were hard to come by. A carcass did not have to have any meat left on it to provide a good meal. An abandoned lion kill, stripped of flesh, still has plenty of nourishment. The marrow from a long bone would provide an adult's daily calorie intake for the cost of just half-an-hour's effort with a hammer-stone. In terms of the energy spent, this was a more economical way of getting food even than harvesting plants, and so if hominids were guided by natural efficiency they would have preferred scavenging to harvesting.

Scavenging also has considerable advantages over hunting, when the meat must be chased, cornered, killed and hauled to a safe place before the hunters can feed. Early humans used less energy by simply picking their food out of a tree or finding it abandoned on the ground. A group of stone-throwing hominids could easily scare a solitary leopard or cheetah away from its kill. There are, in fact, modern models for this behaviour: chimpanzees and baboons, for instance, usurp the kills of cheetahs and leopards, and the Hadza and San (Bushmen) hunter-gatherers of sub-Saharan Africa are both opportunistic scavengers. All of them also hunt small prey with their hands.

SOCIAL COOPERATION

Scavenging might also have contributed to social changes, such as a greater degree of cooperation. If a carcass fed only one individual there would have been competition between hominids for it, but there was, it seems, a surplus of suitable carcasses which promoted food sharing. There might then have been a division of labour: some foraging, others butchering.

There would have been a need for mental maps, too. Modern primates feeding on fruits have mental maps of their home

DAWN OF MAN *Actors play early hominids in a reconstruction of a hunting party at Lake Nakuru, East Africa.*

FIRST SIGN OF SPEECH

A cast from the cranium of one skull found in Kenya and attributed to *Homo habilis* shows that a part of the cortex of the left hemisphere corresponds to an area of the human brain called Broca's area, which is specialised for language. *Homo habilis* is unlikely to have spoken as we can. Even human infants cannot articulate most sounds until after a year old when the voice box or larynx drops into the throat. In apes this never happens. The degree to which the base of the skull is flexed indicates whether the voice box can move down. *Homo habilis* skulls are only slightly flexed so the sounds it could have produced would not have had the full range we hear from ourselves today. Full speech capability is not thought to have evolved until the later stages of human evolution, after 500 000 years ago.

Nevertheless, it is thought that *Homo habilis* could have possessed the beginnings of spoken language, another of the driving forces behind the rapid increase in brain size that marks our evolution.

TALKING HEADS *In a human adult the larynx is positioned in the throat, and the upper part of the throat, mouth and nasal cavity can be used for making sounds; in a chimpanzee the larynx is closed off from the mouth by the tongue. The vocal tract of a human infant resembles the chimpanzee's.*

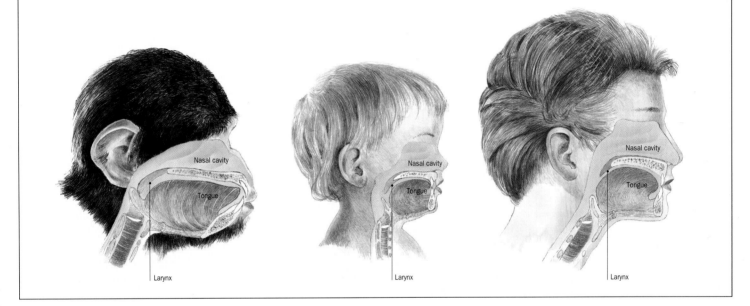

range that allow them to turn up at the right tree at the right time for there to be fruit available. The same kind of mental mapping may have guided hominids to their butchering sites.

Carcasses would have been located by watching and listening. At night the panicked braying of a zebra, for example, the cackle of hyenas, the frightened grunt of a wildebeest or the growling of a pride of lions fighting for a place at table would have given early humans the position of a kill. In the morning, the straight-line flight of a single vulture and the sight of a full-bellied lion leaving the area would have given more clues to the kill's location.

FOOD PREPARATION *Homo habilis used sharp flakes of stone to butcher scavenged carcasses. Special sites were earmarked for this activity.*

Having acquired the corpse, handyman's 'kitchen equipment' was simple but effective. Sharp-edged stone flakes were used to cut away flesh and separate limbs – they were the man-made equivalent of the carnivore's flesh-shearing carnassial teeth. Natural cobbles were used to break marrow bones and skulls.

To handle these tools *Homo habilis* must have had a precision grip. It also retained the ability to climb trees, with a powerful grasping hand. It most probably resorted to trees for sleeping and when escaping the same carnivores from which it scavenged, such as lions.

The fossil bones of a mature, 30-year-old female, found at Olduvai and reported in 1987, provide what may be further evidence of *Homo habilis's* tree-climbing habits. Her arms were long, much like the arms of a female australopithecine. Indeed, they were 95 per cent the length of her legs and hung down to her knees as in modern apes – the

arms of modern humans are only 70 per cent the length of their legs. Her feet were more human-like, and there is speculation that she shifted her weight onto the big toe and used it to shove off from the ground. Apes cannot 'toe-off', but *Homo habilis* probably could, a refinement that separated man's early ancestors from the robust australopithecines with which they shared their living space.

DIMINUTIVE FEMALES

Females were considerably smaller than the males, estimated to have been 4 ft 11 in (1.5 m) tall. This discovery, also made from the Olduvai fossils, was a surprise.

When the handyman fossils were first discovered, palaeoanthropologists considered *Homo habilis* to be the immediate ancestor of modern man, *Homo sapiens*. Since then others have suggested three stages on the evolutionary tree – *Homo habilis, Homo*

BUTCHERING SITES

It was once thought that the early hominids living 2 million years ago were hunter-gatherers, living in temporary camp sites which they occupied for no more than a few weeks at a time, but recent findings have shown that this was not the case. Research on these so-called camp sites in the Olduvai Gorge, for example, has shown that our ancient ancestors returned to the same site repeatedly over a period of five to ten years. Here, they butchered carcasses which they probably scavenged.

Scientists made this discovery by looking at the way the bones of the butchered animals had deteriorated before being buried. Under the influence of sunlight, humidity and bacterial action, bones break down in a particular way. Cracks appear, layers of surface bone peel off and finally the entire bone disintegrates. The process takes about 15 years, but is halted once the bone is buried.

If, then, the hominids followed a nomadic hunter-gatherer lifestyle, moving from camp to camp every few weeks, the fossil bones would all be at the same stage of deterioration having been laid down during the few weeks the hominids stayed at the site – but they are not. In reality, the camp sites show deterioration that must have taken place over a period of five to ten years. During this time, the hominids simply brought their scavenged carcasses, mainly limbs, to the site where they most probably kept a cache of stone butchering tools. These were made from a source of, say, quartzite which might have been collected and carried there from more than 5 miles (8 km) away.

They did not always go to the same site, for large carnivores, such as hyenas, would have been attracted by the smell of meat, and early humans would have wanted to minimise the chances of direct confrontation. Instead they had several sites in their home range and dragged carcasses to the nearest cache of tools. Sleeping sites, say in the safety of trees or cliffs, would have been elsewhere.

A modern equivalent can be seen in chimpanzees, not with

A BUTCHER'S MARKS *The striations on a fragment of bone are the marks made by stone tools used to cut away the flesh.*

meat-eating but with nutcracking. Chimpanzees carry large sticks and stones over short distances to particular nut trees. Here they use these hammer-and-anvil tools to crack tough nuts, such as Kola and Panda nuts. The nutcracking site is visited repeatedly when the nuts are available, and not always by the same band of chimpanzees. Nutshells and the re-usable tools are left behind, just like the bones and stone tools left behind by the early hominids. The only difference between nutcracking and butchering sites is that the hominids had to transport both tools and food to the same site.

It is probable that the tool caching and butchering sites were antecedents to more settled home bases, where fire was used not only to cook but also to frighten away predators, and social interactions began to turn early hominids into more sophisticated social animals.

HOW TO USE TOOLS
A chimpanzee cracking nuts with hammer and anvil demonstrates how early man might have used simple tools, which he probably stored at special feeding sites.

erectus ('upright man') and *Homo sapiens*. *Homo erectus* had a larger brain and bigger body than *Homo habilis* and emerged around 1.8 million years ago.

If the members of *Homo habilis* were midway between the australopithecines and *Homo erectus*, it followed that they should be midway in size. The Olduvai fossil bones, however, suggest that females were no more than 3 ft 4 in (1 m) tall, slightly shorter even than the australopithecine Lucy. Until this discovery scientists had believed in a gradual

GONE FISHING

Early humans may have eaten fish around 2 million years ago. Fish-bone debris at early hominid sites suggests that fish provided protein and fat when other food was in short supply – in the dry season, for instance. They did not use sophisticated harpoons or fish hooks, but simply scooped the fish out of the water just as some African peoples do today. At certain times of the year, fish are easier to catch: when they enter the shallows to spawn, for example. They also become stranded in small, muddy pools in the dry season. By the end of the dry season, fish tend to put on fat reserves ready for spawning, making them especially nutritious at this time of the year. Most early hominids lived close to lakes and rivers, and the remains of fish meals are found at most sites. In the Olduvai Gorge, for example, 4000 fragments of catfish and *Tilapia*, a perch-like fish found in African lakes, have been found near *Homo habilis* and *Homo erectus* remains.

change between species, but here was evidence that the change in size of the females may have been abrupt.

Another intepretation, however, was possible, one that is finding increasing support among experts. According to this the Olduvai female came from a separate, smaller *Homo* species. A number of scientists believe that *Homo habilis* has been a convenient 'waste basket' for pre-human fossils dated around 2 million years ago. The unexpected difference between the two sexes might, they believe, indicate more than one

species present in the fossil record for the same period. The smaller species might have died out and the larger species could well have shown a more gradual change to *Homo erectus*. Important finds of the larger form have been discovered near Lake Turkana – formerly Lake Rudolf – in the Great Rift Valley, and supporters of the two-species theory have ascribed them to a new species, *Homo rudolfensis*.

If, on the other hand, the large males and smaller females really did come from the same species, the difference in size between them suggests certain things about *Homo habilis*'s social habits. Scientists draw a parallel with modern equivalents. Gorillas and orang-utans have large males and small females, whereas chimpanzees and humans, like *Homo erectus*, have males and females that are closer in size. This difference can be linked to social organisation. Gorillas have harems of females dominated by a single silverback male. Orang-utans have a loose social system with solitary males. In both systems there is considerable competition for access to females, a selection pressure which favours big, dominating males. The reduction in size difference seen in chimps, humans and *Homo erectus* suggests more cooperation between males, a factor which coincides with a dietary change towards meat – this makes sense because scavenging and hunting require greater cooperation among the scavengers and hunters than gathering does among the gatherers.

PLACE ON THE TREE

The hypothesis that *Homo habilis* was the ancestor of *Homo erectus* presents a growing number of puzzles. The gap between the australopithecines and *Homo*

STONE TOOLS *These chunks of rock are the 2-million-year-old choppers of* Homo habilis *found in Kenya. They were used for butchering animals.*

erectus is large, and the *habilis* specimens uncovered by palaeoanthropologists show too much variety to bridge it neatly.

Various theories have been put forward. According to one, the small form of *habilis* evolved early, more than 2 million years ago, possibly from *Australopithecus afarensis* (Lucy). The larger form (or *Homo rudolfensis*) evolved later from *Australopithecus africanus*, the fossil species first discovered by Raymond Dart in 1924. Another theory is also founded on the belief that there were two species of *habilis*. On the basis of facial similarities and dental evidence, it suggests that the smaller *habilis* evolved from *Australopithecus africanus* and the larger form was simply another robust australopithecine.

None of the theories provides a satisfactory explanation for the origins of *Homo erectus*, still regarded as the ancestor of modern man. This leaves one thing clear: hominids were making the transition from man-ape to early humans just under 2 million years ago. But the exact line of their descent yet again proves difficult to pin down.

UPRIGHT MAN

Homo erectus was an intrepid explorer. Fossils of 'upright men' have been found in places as far apart as northern China, Indonesia and the Caucasus, as well as in Africa. Homo erectus was also the first of the hunter-stalkers.

From at least 1.8 million years ago and for well over a million years after that, a form of early hominid lived that showed a number of evolutionary firsts: the first signs of cooperative hunting as opposed to opportunistic scavenging; the first use of fire; the first systematic tool-making as opposed to opportunistic stone knapping; the first evidence of seasonal home bases or camp-sites; and the first evidence of hom-inids living outside Africa – across Asia and in Europe.

The first *Homo erectus* skull was found as long ago as 1891 on the Indonesian island of Java. It was discovered and described by the Dutch doctor Eugène Dubois, and since his remarkable find many specimens, dated between 1.8 and 0.1 million years old, have been found in Java, China and Africa. Dubois gave his find the name '*Pithecanthropus erectus*', but today it and related specimens have been dubbed *Homo erectus*.

It had a large brain with teeth that were arranged in a distinctly human fashion. Unlike modern humans, the forehead was low and sloping. But it was similar in height to modern humans, although more strongly built than we are, and like us it was a habitual 'biped'.

A SUDDEN ARRIVAL

Homo erectus's appearance on Earth seems to have been remarkably 'sudden' on the geological timescale. It has, for example, a number of much more advanced features than its immediate predecessors, *Homo habilis* and the australopithecines. This apparently sudden evolutionary leap may simply reflect the poor fossil record of the place where it emerged – possibly even outside Africa. Or it may be an example of a kind of spurt in human evolution known as 'punctuated equilibrium'. This is usually put down to abrupt changes in climate and vegetation after millions of years of very gradual change.

From 10 until 3 million years ago – the so-called 'golden era' – the global climate was relatively warm, but then it began to deteriorate. About 2.6 million years ago (around the same time that the earliest-known representative of the genus *Homo* was alive), ice built up at the poles, and the climate became cyclical – periods of icy glaciation across northern Europe and Asia and North America alternating with short, warmer interglacial periods. In Africa a warm, moist climate changed to cooler, more arid conditions. Vegetation was sparser and hardier, and hominids had to be more mobile and to broaden their diet in order to find enough food to survive.

Although these climatic and vegetation changes provide an explanation for many aspects of early hominid life, they do not tell the full story. Here, volcanologists (scientists who study volcanoes) enter the scene. About 1.6 million years ago, according to German researchers from the University of Karlsruhe, there was intense volcanic activity along the East African Rift. Around the same time there was another change. While the climate continued to cool and became drier, volcanoes were blowing their tops and the vegetation thinned out. The large herds of game in eastern and southern Africa also diminished. First, the gracile australop-

STANDING UPRIGHT *Homo erectus had several features – such as a prominent nose – that are also characteristic of modern man.*

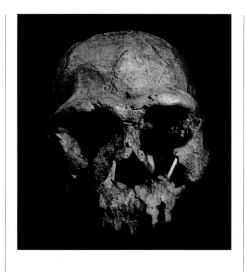

ithecines, mainly dependent on fruits, nuts and seeds, became extinct. Later, *Homo habilis*, the scavenger of surplus meat, followed the same path to extinction.

The time of plenty was over. Early man had to set about actively seeking high-energy food and *Homo erectus* emerged as a true, stalking hunter. About 1 million years ago, the robust australopithecines disappeared. Whether *Homo erectus* had anything to do with their demise is unknown. Was there competition for food which the superior-brained *Homo* won, or did *Homo erectus* give *Australopithecus* an evolutionary push by carving him up for his dinner?

The shift to hunting coincides with man's probable move out of Africa into the rest of the Old World, a pattern shown by two other African hunters, the lion and the cheetah, which had a much larger range in historic times – lions, for example, lived in western Asia until the 18th century. *Homo erectus* had moved from a mainly herbivorous diet, with occasional meat, to a mainly carnivorous one.

Carnivores will always represent a tiny minority – about 1 per cent – of the biomass, the living organisms in a particular area. Inevitably, the bulk of carnivores' diet comes from herbivores which, in order to survive, have to be far more numerous than the animals that prey on them. The herbivores, in their turn, feed off a still more plentiful plant life. For these reasons combined with the shrinking herds of game, the new, partly carnivorous hominid had to reduce its numbers, or shrink in body size, or spread itself more thinly on the ground.

Herbivores are confined to the places where their food plants and sufficient water are concentrated, and they either stay put or follow a cyclical migration pattern, like the wildebeest of East Africa do today; they follow the rain and new grass. A carnivore has greater flexibility: it can move from one herbivore centre to the next, preying on the animals feeding there. Having been forced into hunting, some groups of *Homo erectus* had to move a very long way indeed – out of Africa altogether. By a million years ago *Homo erectus* was in south-eastern and eastern Asia and probably in Europe. There is fossil evidence that groups lived in China until about 200 000 years ago and in Java until as recently as 100 000 years ago.

Homo erectus probably carried on evolving. An examination of the skulls, jaws and teeth of 92 specimens from all parts of its range and from early, middle and late dates, by researchers from the University of Michigan at Ann Arbor, suggest many changes occurred during the million years and more the species was alive. With few exceptions the changes seem to have moved gradually to a more modern profile: cranial capacity expanded, while tooth and jaw size shrank.

TURKANA BOY

The earliest *Homo erectus* fossils, of a boy about 11 years old, were found at Nariokotome on the west side of Lake Turkana in 1984, by the fossil-hunter Kamoya Kimeu.

THE HUNT *A group of* Homo erectus *cooperate in stalking game at a water hole.*

FOSSIL-HUNTERS
Palaeontologist Richard Leakey with Kamoya Kimeu, who has spotted many of the valuable hominid fossils at excavations at East Turkana (above) in northern Kenya.

The fossilised bones of other individuals had previously been found on the east side in 1971 and later. The bones of the young boy, however, dated to about 1.7 million years ago, represent the most complete hominid skeleton of such antiquity so far discovered and they give some insight into growth and development in early humans.

Essentially, given a baseball cap to cover his prominent brow ridges and low brain case, the boy might be able to pass in the street for a modern boy. However, there were plenty of differences. The boy's brain size was about 55 cu in (900 cm³), compared with 67 cu in (1100 cm³) in later humans. The cranium or brain case was long and low, and the bone thicker than in earlier hominids. The face was short but wide, and the nose was more like a modern nose with the nostrils pointing down. The shape of the nose, like the nose of the modern camel, would have allowed water vapour in exhaled air to condense and be reabsorbed: an adaptation to arid conditions. There were pronounced brow ridges above the eyes. The spinal cord was thinner than in modern humans, which ties in with a smaller brain, and the rib cage was conical-shaped like that of an ape, rather than barrel-shaped like a modern human.

COOKING, PROTECTION AND WARMTH: THE USES OF FIRE

Evidence for the earliest use of fire comes from the Swartkrans cave in South Africa, dated to 1.5 million years ago. Of 60 000 fossil fragments found in the cave about 270 show obvious signs of having been burned. The scientists from the Transvaal Museum in Pretoria who made the discovery checked that the blackening of the bones was, indeed, the result of charring by comparing the burnt fossil bones with burnt pieces of modern hartebeest bones.

The modern antelope bones were heated to camp fire temperatures, using the branches of white stinkwood (a common tree in the vicinity) and then allowed to cool slowly. Both the modern hartebeest bones and the fossil bones were similarly blackened and showed comparable damage to the cellular structure of the bone.

Whether the ancient camp fire was made by *Homo erectus* or *Australopithecus robustus*, both of which occupied the Swartkrans cave, is unknown, although the big-brained *Homo* is a clear favourite. The burned bones found in the cave included wildebeest-sized antelopes, zebra, warthog, baboon and the charred remains of *Australopithecus robustus* – evidence, perhaps, that *Homo erectus* found his australopithecine cousin good to eat.

The charring of the bones is significant. A wood-based camp fire is quite hot and by the time the bones became charred any meat attached to them would have been burnt and inedible. It is thought, then, that the meat was removed – cooked or uncooked – and the stripped bones tossed into the fire to help to keep our ancestors warm on a cold winter

Camp-fire Rendezvous
San foragers (Bushmen) in the Kalahari gather around a camp fire at night, which both keeps them warm and wards off predators.

night in the Transvaal. The fire also burned up any waste which would have attracted scavengers and predators.

It is unclear whether the fire was lit for cooking or whether it was simply there for protection and warmth, but there is evidence that is was a frequent activity. Protection would have been important. Leopards were probably a constant threat, and they are afraid of fire. Early man only had to watch their behaviour in the face of bush fires to know that fire was a useful deterrent.

The evidence for the deliberate use of fire at Swartkrans is fairly convincing, but there is an alternative explanation. Our early ancestors could have been returning to the cave with the partially burned carcasses of animals that had been caught in bush fires. Fires would have been just as common as they are today. In this way, early man would have discovered the delights of cooked meat and used the natural disaster, probably triggered by an electrical storm or volcanic eruption, to stock his larder.

A student at the University of Cape Town once explored the possibility. He arranged with park rangers to be present at a controlled burn and placed a supermarket chicken in the path of the flames. The meat was cooked to perfection. The absence of a series of hearths in the cave deposits, and no evidence of fire-lighting tools, such as bow-drills which came much later, suggest that the second interpretation is credible.

At Chesowanja near Lake Baringo in Kenya, British, American and Kenyan scientists discovered chips of stone, broken and scratched bones and burnt clay. The evidence suggests an actual camp fire, and a date of 1.4 million years ago makes it one of the oldest-known controlled uses of fire. The scorching of the clay is too deep for a bush fire and inconsistent with lightning strikes or volcanic activity, but is just right for a camp fire. Indeed, the scientists were able to work out the temperature of this ancient fire by looking at the magnetism of the rocks.

When a rock is heated it loses its natural magnetism, and, as it cools, it takes on new magnetism from the Earth's magnetic field at the time. If a sample of the rock is placed in a coil, which neutralises the Earth's present magnetic field, and is heated and the change in its magnetism recorded, the temperature of the rock at the time of the ancient fire can be worked out. In this way, the Chesowanja rock was shown to have been heated to a temperature of 400°C (752°F), the maximum temperature to be expected from a camp fire of burning wood.

Until these finds, the first convincing evidence that early man used fire came in the 1930s from excavations in Zhoukoudian in China. Burnt bones of deer, charcoal, fire-branded chipped stone artefacts and thick layers of ash were found alongside the fossil remains of *Homo erectus*. The remains were dated to about 400 000 to 300 000 years ago.

STONE KNAPPING *Simple tools were made by striking one stone against another to chip off flakes that were sharp enough to use for cutting.*

The top of the femur was also different from that in modern man. The femur fits into the pelvis with a ball-and-socket joint, and its shape is linked to the gait of its owner. The ball in the modern human leg sits on a short neck at the top of the femur, and this fits into a broad pelvis. The australopithecine pattern had a small ball on a long neck, fitting with a narrow pelvis. Turkana boy, however, has a large ball on a long neck, with a narrow pelvis: a mixture of man-ape and human features.

He was surprisingly tall at 5 ft 4 in (1.6 m) and might have grown to 6 ft (1.8 m) when adult. He would, however, have been quite small at birth. In modern monkeys and apes, the head of a newborn infant is half the size of an adult's. The adult pelvis of a female *Homo erectus*, however, is far too narrow to accommodate a baby with a head 50 per cent the size of an adult's. The baby would have been born earlier in its development than with monkeys and apes, with a maximum head size of 23 cu in (377 cm^3). It had to increase its brain size by two and a half times after birth to reach the adult size.

LOOKING AFTER BABY

Turkana boy would have spent more time growing up than his predecessors, with a period of parental care and a greater chance for social learning, another move in the direction of modern human patterns. To provide all this, his mother needed a high-quality supply of food which could have been obtained only by efficient food gathering, including the hunting or scavenging of meat, and food sharing.

Homo erectus made stone tools, struck from cobbles, for cutting, scraping, digging or butchering. Then, about 1.4 million years ago, a new type of large, symmetrically shaped stone implement entered the prehistoric tool kit. It was a tear-shaped hand axe. The first examples to be found came from Saint-Acheul on the outskirts of Amiens in northern France and so tools of this kind are referred to as Acheulian. Some scientists have speculated that the hand axes might have been projectile weapons thrown like a discus, though the present consensus is that they were used for butchery. More significantly, there is evidence that axes from different regions of the Old World had local styles: some resembled giant almonds, others were more oval-shaped and some were triangular. It seems that for the first time early humans were consciously fashioning tools that fitted patterns established by local tradition, rather than simply chipping away at cobbles until they happened to take on a convenient shape.

The latest excavation to yield tools belonging to *Homo erectus* is behind the main railway station in Würzburg, Bavaria. Early

TOOL SITE *Half-buried stone tools were discovered in this excavation in Kenya.*

humans lived there about 800 000 years ago, and they fed on deer and wild cattle. The bones found show that marrow from long bones and the brains from skulls were extracted using stone tools, and that meat was tenderised before it was eaten. Evidence for marrow extraction comes from a fossilised bison's leg, with an aperture in it made with a heavy blunt instrument, such as a piece of stag's antler or an elephant bone. Lower jawbones might well have been used as saws, the German scientists suggest.

FOR THE CHOP *This pointed stone hand axe, illustrated here life-size, has the two carefully honed 'faces' that are typical of the Acheulian tool industry.*

The site, now high and dry on a vine-covered hillside, was once next to a gap that provided the access point to a watering site on the River Main. The river has since changed its course, but 800 000 years ago herds of animals would have made their way through the gap, from the dry steppe behind, and headed for the water.

Homo erectus was waiting for them. Some cattle and deer became stuck in lowland mires and were set upon, both by early man and other predators. An elephant's foot bone, for example, shows signs of having been chewed by a sabre-toothed cat, and a piece of cattle bone has the bite marks of hyenas. Working together in groups, the hominids would have been able to see off their competitors and take the food for themselves.

LEARNING LANGUAGE

From the fossils that have been discovered so far, it is possible to speculate about the social system of *Homo erectus*. The key is in the size difference between the males and the females. Most previous hominids had large males which were up to twice the size of the females, indicating some degree of competition between males for access to the females for breeding – larger, stronger males would have been more successful. *Homo erectus* males, however, are no more than 20-30 per cent bigger than the females, indicating a reduction in competition between males and the formation of cooperative social groupings. There is the possibility that these groupings encouraged the use of speech for communication. Another possibility is that the early humans used their hands and communicated by some kind of sign language.

This very human-like hominid has always been thought of as the direct ancestor of modern man, but, as with *Homo habilis*, there is speculation that more than one species is represented in the fossil record. Might the 'younger' Asian forms, for example, have died out during the last half-a-million years, whereas the 'older' African forms continued to evolve in the direction of *Homo sapiens*? The assumption is understandably controversial. The argument runs that just because all the specimens have roughly the same sized brains, it does not mean that they all belong to the same species.

Homo erectus, like most species, reveals a number of 'derived' characters, features absent from the ancestral stock, but developed by later generations of the same species and kept by their descendants. The characters that were there from the start are known as 'primitive'. When the 'derived' and 'primitive' characters from the list of attributes assigned to *Homo erectus* are analysed, it is found that the 'derived' characters are present mainly in the Asian species, where there is no link to *Homo sapiens* – the line simply became extinct. The derived characters include an angling of the cranium which creates a bony ridge on the top of the head, a groove in the bone just behind the ear, and a bony swelling at the back of the head.

The African species, without these derived features, but with a full complement of primitive features might well have evolved into the European archaic form of *Homo sapiens* and thus to modern humans. The counter-argument holds that it is just these sorts of anatomical differences that one would expect to see in such a widely spread population. In other words, even at this time in human evolution, just as things seem to have settled down, they are, in fact, as vague and confused as ever.

One British researcher from Liverpool University takes things even farther. He has suggested that there were three species of *Homo* living in Africa at the same time. There was the relatively small-brained *Homo habilis*, the group with larger brains but large teeth named *Homo rudolfensis* and a group christened *Homo ergaster*. *Homo ergaster* continued the more primitive line from which the *Homo erectus* of Asia had evolved. According to him, all three African species shared a common ancestor, but only *Homo ergaster* gave rise to modern man, *Homo sapiens*.

A third view steps back from the business of assigning species names to particular fossils altogether, and looks for related groups which are linked by general anatomical features without sharp breaks between them. They have been called 'grades'. The story goes that an *Australopithecus* grade merged into a grade containing *Homo erectus* fossils, which then blended into a *Homo sapiens* grade, the grade which contains our own species.

THE NEANDERTHALS

The Neanderthals were almost like us, but not quite.

They were immensely strong, intelligent and skilled hunters.

In the end, however, they lost the evolutionary race to

their still more successful cousins, Homo sapiens *– ourselves.*

The Neanderthals lived in Europe, the Near East and Asia from about 230 000 to 30 000 years ago. Traditionally, *Homo neanderthalensis* – named after the gorge-like Neander Valley, lying 7 miles (11 km) east of Düsseldorf in Germany, where Neanderthal fossils were found in the 19th century – has been thought of as the slouching, dimwitted brute of the ancient world, but that was the result of a mistake. In the early 20th century a French palaeontologist, Marcellin Boule, reconstructed an arthritic skeleton without realising how unrepresentative it was – and the unflattering profile that resulted stuck. In reality, the Neanderthals were not much different from us, although decidedly more robust. Their skeletons, with rather short lower legs and arms, are reminiscent of modern peoples adapted to cold climates, such as the Saami (Lapps) and Inuit (Eskimos). A thick, stocky body retains heat better than a more gangling one, losing less from its smaller surface area. The Neanderthals' very large, broad noses warmed and moistened cold, dry air. They were the first humans to adapt to colder climates, occupying lands as far north as Britain.

They were powerful enough to bring down game. Heavy bones indicate large muscles so that any ordinary Neanderthal would have tested the might of many latter-day body builders. They also had larger heads and larger brains than modern man – which does not mean that they were cleverer than us, since bulkier bodies need larger brains to co-ordinate them. They had heavy brow ridges over the eyes, receding cheekbones and a receding lower jaw. The forehead was minimal, the brain case sloping low at the back, but they were far from brutish.

They were intelligent enough to manufacture sophisticated stone tools, hunted co-operatively, possessed a rudimentary language, buried their dead and looked after their sick. A skull from a cave site in Croa-tia, for example, shows signs of a head wound which had healed. The wound would have been extremely debilitating and the victim must have required help from others in order to survive.

For modern scholars, Neanderthals remain an enigma. They were intelligent and resourceful creatures living and surviving in harsh climates for tens of thousands of years, yet about 30 000 years ago they disappeared. For scholars in the last century, in uproar over the new evolutionary theories, they were vital scientific evidence of man's ancient past.

THE FOSSILS

The year was 1856, and the place the Neander Valley. It was a beauty spot then, though today much of the valley has been destroyed by limestone quarrying. Indeed, the first fossils in the valley were uncovered by quarrymen in the Feldhofer Cave, and taken to a school in neighbouring Elberfeld. Initially, the scientific community dismissed the specimens, 14 pieces in all, as nothing of any

NEANDERTHAL *The powerful, thick-set Neanderthal was well adapted to explore, exploit and survive in the colder regions of Europe.*

EARLIEST EVIDENCE *These bones, including a skullcap, leg, hip and arm, were the first evidence of an evolutionary link between apes and humans.*

great significance. They came from the same skeleton which had a broken arm and signs of arthritis throughout. It was variously described as that of a 'poor idiot or hermit' and a 'misshapen freak'. The bowed leg bones even prompted one scientist to suggest the skeleton was that of a Mongolian cavalryman who had suffered from rickets. It was a number of years before their true importance was realised.

Once that happened, however, they became prime evidence to support Darwin's newly emerging theory of evolution. Neanderthal man was proffered as the 'missing link', and many more fossils began to be discovered in several other parts of Europe to help the cause. The next to appear were in Belgium where two skeletons similar to those at Neanderthal were found in the Cave of Spy alongside stone implements and the bones of subarctic animals. The biggest haul was unearthed in a cave near the village of Krapina in Croatia, where parts of at least 25 skeletons were found at the turn of the cen-

tury. Two much earlier finds – from Belgium, unearthed in 1830, and Gibraltar, discovered in 1848 – which had long lain unrecognised were also finally identified for what they were.

We know as little about how the Neanderthals appeared as we do about how they disappeared. It is thought that they evolved, as did modern man, from *Homo erectus* who moved from Africa into the Mediterranean

region and on to the rest of Eurasia between a million and 700 000 years ago. Populations of Neanderthals were probably never large. Estimates put their numbers at no more than tens of thousands at any one time. A second invasion of Europe and Asia about 40 000 years ago, this time by an early form of modern man, coincides with the Neanderthals' disappearance from the fossil record. Whether they lost the competition for living space, were wiped out by some deadly disease brought in by modern man (just as smallpox would later be carried with devastating results to the New World by Europeans), or interbred to extinction is not known.

NEANDERTHAL FOREBEARS

Some light is currently being thrown on the Neanderthals' origins by fossils being recovered from the floor of a deep cave in Spain. About 160 ft (50 m) below the Sierra de Atapuerca of northern Spain is a deep hole known as La Sima de Los Huesos. Here, Spanish anthropologists and archaeologists are uncovering many fossil bones, from at
continued on page 58

SURPRISE ATTACK *Depicted in this 1909 engraving as a dimwitted, ape-like creature, Neanderthal man was in reality a successful hunter-gatherer.*

NEANDERTHAL LIVING *A group*
of Neanderthals skin and
butcher the carcass of an
animal. Evidence suggests that
Neanderthals hunted in
well-coordinated parties.
They were armed with spears
and with stone weapons, such
as the one being made in the
foreground.

least 23 individuals, estimated to be about 300 000 years old. From three complete skulls the researchers have found that the face of these hominids projected forwards like that of Neanderthals and the back of the head had a pit in the middle as did Neanderthals. They are clearly pre-Neanderthals, forerunners of 'classical' Neanderthals.

Why so many bones should be found at the excavation site is a mystery. The idea that the cave might have been a carnivore's den is rejected by some because the bones are said to have no teeth marks on them. A few researchers have suggested that the cave was previously open and the entrance collapsed, trapping an entire group of hominids inside. Others have suggested a catastrophic flood which washed through the cave system engulfing an entire community. A third explanation holds that the community lived at the entrance of the cave and disposed of their dead corpses by throwing them down the deep shaft.

Evidence of the next stage in Neanderthal evolution, and signs of true Neanderthals dating from 230 000 to 150 000 years ago, came from northern France. At Biache-Saint-Vaast construction workers chanced upon the remains of two skulls in 1976 when they were digging out the foundations for a new steel mill. The fossil bones were accompanied by many flint implements and animal bones, mainly cave bears and aurochs (cow-like animals believed to be the forerunners of modern domestic cattle). It looked as if they had discovered a Neanderthal butchering site, and the animals these ancient hominids were butchering were powerful and dangerous. Neanderthals must have got together in well-coordinated hunting parties to be able to tackle such beasts.

About 180 000 years ago, the Neanderthal story goes into temporary eclipse as ice spread across Europe and a period of glaciation took a hold. Only a few fossils have been found from the next 50 000 years. Then life re-established itself as the ice retreated.

The Neanderthals somehow survived the worst of the Ice Ages and about 130 000 years ago, when the climate warmed again, they reappeared. The Krapina specimens from Croatia were from this period, and the bones of young rhinoceroses found near the hominid remains may bear witness to the Neanderthals' hunting prowess – they are also evidence of the warm-climate animals that lived there. The Neanderthals would have had to outwit and outmanoeuvre the mother rhino in order to capture her baby.

There is evidence to suggest that taking the young of large and powerful animals was a common hunting ploy, but not the only one.

At the time, Neanderthal men would have been competing with other hunters, such as lions and wolves, for food. But where these other beasts of prey target the old, the infirm and the injured, the Neanderthals

FIRST JEWELLERY

At a Neanderthal site at Tata in northern Hungary the polished ivory tooth of a baby mammoth, thought to be about 50 000 years old, was not a practical tool but a piece of primitive art. What it represents is unclear: whether a shaman's amulet, for instance, or a healer's charm. But it is an indication that Neanderthals had symbolic or ritualistic objects.

could tackle the large and powerful – even mammoths. They thus successfully exploited an alternative food source. They did not have sophisticated weapons, so they probably surrounded the prey, causing it to panic. They might have used bogs and other natural traps to corner panicking animals, killing them with spears. An 8 ft (2.4 m) wooden spear was discovered alongside fossil elephant bones in a bog in Germany.

Smashed bones alongside skulls with cut-marks, resembling those seen on butchered animals, indicate that the Croatian Neanderthals might have butchered each other. Whether this was the result of some kind of ritual or whether they were cannibals who actually ate each other is uncertain and difficult to prove. Some scientists prefer to think that they honoured their dead, while others believe these ancient men let nothing go

LA VACHE CAVE *An engraving of a bison's head on bone and decorated antlers have been found in this cave, occupied during the Upper Palaeolithic.*

RIGHT-HANDED NEANDERTHALS

In an ingenious experiment carried out by scientists in Madrid in 1988, it was established that Neanderthals were mainly right-handed. The clue was in the pattern of scratches on the front teeth – the canines and incisors. The scratches were thought to have been made accidentally as meat was cut, held between the teeth, with a stone tool. The idea was tested when one of the team was fitted with a sports' gum shield into which a porcelain copy of the teeth of Neanderthals had been fixed. The researcher then held meat between his Neanderthal dentures and cut it with a specially made flint tool held in the right hand. The scratches on the porcelain copies matched those on the teeth from an-

cient skulls. The teeth from many skulls were examined microscopically and most showed the same pattern, indicating that their owners were right-handed. One skull, however, showed that its owner was left-handed.

During the same year scientists in the USA examined Neanderthal teeth from Croatia and revealed artificial grooves on the back teeth. It is thought that these indicate the use of toothpicks to keep the gaps between teeth clear of food debris. Similar grooves had been found and reported in 1911 on Neanderthal

teeth from France. They have also been seen on specimens of *Homo habilis* from Omo in Ethiopia, dating to 1.84 million years ago, and on *Homo erectus* and archaic *Homo sapiens* from China, North Africa, Spain and Russia. The grooves are found, too, on more recent specimens of modern man who lived in Mesolithic, Neolithic and Bronze Age times. The consistent location of the grooves throughout time and the unchanging longitudinal polish

and striations suggests a prolonged back-and-forth movement with an inflexible object, like a stick. Amerindians, Australian Aborigines, Canary Islanders and Upper Dynastic Egyptians show similar grooves in their teeth.

DINNER TIME *One Neanderthal tucks in, while his companion grips a piece of meat with his teeth as he skins it.*

to waste and ate meat and marrow from their recently dead. The cut-marks on both human and animal remains are the same, and are found on the bones of specimens that lived many thousands of years apart.

THE DECLINE

About 100 000 years ago the ice began to creep south again, and another Ice Age may have driven some Neanderthals into the Middle East, where they lived alongside early modern man. Both hunted the same animals and lived in similar ways. Modern

man showed little sign of a more advanced lifestyle than his Neanderthal cousins until about 50 000 years ago. At this point a divergence appears: fine blades and weapons that could be thrown begin to be found at the living sites of modern man, but not at those of Neanderthals. Why such a shift should have taken place is a mystery. Some 10 000 years later modern man moved into Europe and the Neanderthals disappeared.

More slender, less robust Neanderthal bones have been discovered at Vindija in Croatia, suggesting that some interbreeding

may have occurred amongst groups of Neanderthals and early modern humans. For the rest, the fossil record indicates that either the fluctuating climate 40-30 000 years ago or advancing modern humans drove the Neanderthals to the margins of Europe, including the tip of the Iberian Peninsula. Here remains have been found in sea caves along the coast of the Costa del Sol and around Gibraltar. They hung on until about 29 000 years ago – for some reason, they never crossed the few miles back to Africa. Then they became extinct.

THE ARRIVAL OF MODERN MAN

The transition from upright man to modern man was slow and gradual. The process was finally completed by about 40 000 years ago when Cro-Magnon man – modern Homo sapiens *– was conquering the Old World and moving into the New.*

Elephants, rhinoceroses and other such beasts roamed large stretches of northern Europe from 500 000 to 250 000 years ago. The climate was generally a little hotter then than it is today and mammals had spread up from southern lands, colonising the less crowded territories to the north. Among them were early humans, more evolved than *Homo erectus*, showing a number of the characteristics that would later mark out both the Neanderthals and modern man, *Homo sapiens*.

Hominid remains, possibly of an ancestor of the Neanderthals, have been found as far north as Swanscombe, on the banks of the River Thames near London. The Swanscombe fossil consists of three parts of the back of a skull, and these show that the skull's owner, a woman, had lost the small brain of *Homo erectus*. Indeed, calculations show that she had a brain-size of 80 cu in (1300 cm^3) – compared with the average in modern humans of 82 cu in (1350 cm^3). The same site also yielded some carefully hewn stone axes which are the most sophisticated to be found from this period.

THE ARK AND THE CANDELABRA

The transition between *Homo erectus* and *Homo sapiens*, and how exactly the Neanderthals fit into it, has its obscurities like most of the rest of the story of mankind.

There are two extreme views. One, the 'Noah's Ark' hypothesis (also known as the 'Garden of Eden' or 'Out of Africa' hypothesis), maintains that modern *Homo sapiens* – mankind as we know it – emerged from Africa, and nowhere else, about 100 000 years ago. But the process that led from *Homo erectus* to this modern human had started many thousands of years earlier. In different parts of the Old World indigenous populations of *erectus* had independently been evolving in a direction that led to creatures possessing a number of the qualities of modern man. These hominids, whose remains have been found in places as diverse as Jinniu Shan in northern China,

CRO-MAGNON MAN *Such was the size and shape of early modern man that he could walk the streets today and not look out of place. Right: The 'Out of Africa' (bottom) and the 'Candelabra' (top) hypotheses show two possible ways in which modern man might have evolved.*

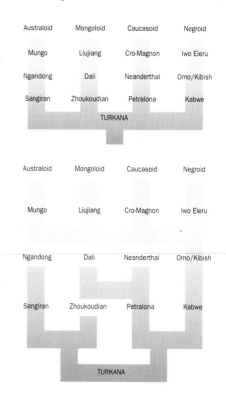

Australoid	Mongoloid	Caucasoid	Negroid
Mungo	Liujiang	Cro-Magnon	Iwo Eleru
Ngandong	Dali	Neanderthal	Omo/Kibish
Sangiran	Zhoukoudian	Petralona	Kabwe

TURKANA

Australoid	Mongoloid	Caucasoid	Negroid
Mungo	Liujiang	Cro-Magnon	Iwo Eleru
Ngandong	Dali	Neanderthal	Omo/Kibish
Sangiran	Zhoukoudian	Petralona	Kabwe

TURKANA

Broken Hill in Zambia, Arago in France and Petralona in Greece, are sometimes labelled 'archaic *Homo sapiens*', and sometimes assigned to their own species, *Homo heidelbergensis* – after a fossil jaw from one of them, found near Heidelberg in Germany in 1907. In Europe and western Asia they led in turn to the Neanderthals. The most successful group, however, were those who evolved in Africa, leading eventually to modern *Homo sapiens* who went on to colonise the rest of the world, gradually replacing his less successful cousins, such as the Neanderthals.

The other view, known as the 'candelabra' hypothesis, maintains, like the 'Out of Africa' theory, that different groups of *Homo erectus* living in different parts of the Old

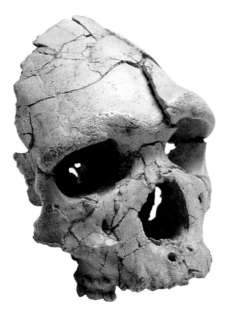

World evolved more or less independently into archaic forms of *Homo sapiens*. Where it differs from the 'Out of Africa' theory is in arguing that all, or most, of these archaic groups continued to evolve into fully fledged modern humans. Throughout the process neighbouring groups interbred, bringing continuity across the different populations.

ARAGO MAN *Showing features of* Homo erectus *and* H. sapiens, *this skull is thought to be an intermediate stage between ancient and modern humans. Below: Arago man lived in limestone caves in the foothills of the French Pyrenees.*

TOOLS AND WEAPONS

The modern *Homo sapiens* of the Upper Palaeolithic were making sophisticated tools and weapons. Where the toolmaking industry of the European Lower Palaeolithic, starting about 1 million years ago, had no more than a dozen identifiable implements, the Middle Palaeolithic toolmakers of 200 000 years ago manufactured closer to 40 types of tool. The Upper Palaeolithic, beginning 40 000 years ago, had nearer to 100 distinct tools and weapons. Evolution in toolmaking was relatively static for thousands of years but by about 35 000 years ago, in Europe, there was a new revolution. For about 30 000 years no fewer than four distinct periods of technological

IMPROVING TOOLS *A flint hatchet (below) and small, handheld bifaces (bottom) of the Lower Palaeolithic show far less refinement in carving and polishing than a bifacial spear blade of the Upper Palaeolithic (centre).*

transition occurred, an unprecedented rate of change. Stone tools were more delicately fashioned. Bone, ivory and antler were used for the first time, and tools were adorned with carvings of the animals they were designed to kill and butcher.

Middle Palaeolithic tools are characterised by the Levallois technique of toolmaking, named after a suburb of Paris where the first of these tools was found. The tools are manufactured by striking a core stone at an angle on an anvil stone. This produced a relatively thin flake, flat on one side and concave on the other. The Neanderthals' tools – known as Mousterian after the fossil site at Le Moustier in the Périgord region of France – were of this type and changed very little over 200 000 years. The characteristic tool shape of the Upper Palaeolithic is the blade, a flake at least twice as long as it is wide. Some are incredibly delicate, such as the 8 in (20 cm) Solutrean blades, named after Solutré in central

France where an early example was found. These are shaped like laurel leaves and are sometimes thin enough to be translucent.

Evidence is most abundant in Europe because most research into this period in the emergence of man has happened there. The Europeans followed and hunted reindeer, a favourite prey, and attacked using weapons such as the *atlatl* or spear-thrower and may have had the bow

SEWING NEEDLES *Needles fashioned out of tusks and antlers were used to stitch together garments made from dressed hides.*

and arrow. Many weapons are things of beauty with finely dressed blades and points. Tools were used for engraving bone and ivory for ornamentation, drilling eyes in bone needles, or carving bone fish-hooks.

SPEAR-THROWER *A rod-like spear-thrower made of reindeer antler enabled hunters to hurl the projectile with great power over considerable distances.*

Proponents of this view trace a direct line from European *Homo erectus* through the Neanderthals to modern Europeans.

A third possibility involves a combination of these two schemes. It allows for an isolated origin for fully modern man, followed by migration and interbreeding with local populations of archaic *sapiens* which had evolved separately.

TIMES OF CHANGE

The actual timing of the transition from *Homo erectus* to archaic *Homo sapiens* to the Neanderthals and modern *Homo sapiens* is no less confusing. In the summer of 1995 a find of fossil hominid remains, estimated to be about 780 000 years old, was reported from the Gran Dolina Cave in the Sierra de Atapuerca of northern Spain. The remains were of four individuals – two adults, a 15-year-old and an infant of three or four years old. They are the oldest-known Europeans, possible ancestors of the Neanderthals.

At Boxgrove near Chichester in England the shinbone and teeth of an archaic *Homo sapiens* (*Homo heidelbergensis*) turned up in a quarry. The find was estimated to be 500 000 years old. Boxgrove man was thought to be about 6 ft (1.8 m) tall, and weighed about 176 lb (80 kg). Remains of an ancient rhinoceros at the site, with a wound in the scapula, indicated that Boxgrove man was a hunter rather than a scavenger. Moreover, bringing down such a creature would have required a degree of cooperation with others. The oldest antler hammer in the world, used to refine the stone tools used by Boxgrove man, was also found nearby.

Other finds have been dated to more recent times. A skull from Petralona in Greece, dated to 400 000 to 300 000 years ago, is a mosaic of *erectus* and more modern features. The brow ridges are ancient, while the large, rounded cranium is modern. Parts of a more complete skull were found at Steinheim in Germany. Found in a gravel pit in 1933, this has several teeth preserved in the upper jaw, but the lower jaw is missing. The brain capacity has been estimated at between 67 and 73 cu in (1100 and 1200 cm^3), slightly smaller than in the Swanscombe woman. It has brow ridges, but smaller teeth than *Homo erectus*,

another trend towards modern man. Fossils from Arago in the French Pyrenees, dated to 250 000 years ago, consist of a face and forehead, and several lower jaws. They, too, show transitional features between *Homo erectus*, Neanderthals and modern *Homo sapiens* – a brow ridge like the Steinheim skull but with

---

THE BLADE INDUSTRY

A 33 000-year-old mine was found in 1984 near cliffs on the western side of the Nile Valley at Nazlet Khater in Egypt. Here horizontal trenches and vertical shafts had been dug to gain access to beds containing cobbles of chert, a variety of silica used for making stone tools. Some shafts were enlarged at their base to form bell pits, while tunnelling resulted in short galleries. Many artefacts were found at the site, including burins (engraving tools), bifacial (double-edged) axes and end scrapers. The skeleton of an early modern man was discovered in a grave nearby. Until this discovery, the earliest-known chert mines had been 10 000 years old.

---

a more modern face.

Another find was made at Fontechevade in France. Here, an ancient cave site occupied by successive groups of early humans revealed at its lowest, oldest level parts of two hominid skulls, primitive tools and the bones of rhinos, deer and bear. One of the skulls is estimated to have enclosed a brain of about 85 cu in (1400 cm^3). It is a clear example of archaic *Homo sapiens*.

BROKEN HILL AND THE OMO RIVER

In 1921 a miner at Broken Hill in what was then Northern Rhodesia (now Zambia) discovered a skull and lower limb bone which clearly came from a human-like creature that marked the gradual transition in Africa from *Homo erectus* to archaic and then modern *Homo sapiens*. It had brow ridges and thick buttresses around the eyes, but a large brain with a capacity of about 80 cu in (1300 cm^3). More limb bones, found in 1925, were added to the earlier find and these showed a number of similarities to those of modern man.

Other similar fragments of skulls and jaws have been found in South Africa: at Hopefield near Saldanha Bay, and in a cave at Makapansgat, known as the Cave of Hearths.

Dating these fossils has not been easy. At first, comparisons were made between the stone tools found near the bones and their counterparts of known dates in Europe. This gave an age of no more than 30 000 years old. At the time, however, it was not appreciated that tool technology in Africa was much more advanced than in Europe and so other methods of dating were sought, such as isotope dating of sediments associated with other African stone tool sites. In the end the dates of the Broken Hill and Hopefield sites were pushed back to 300 000 years ago, indicating an *erectus-sapiens* transition taking place at that time in Africa as well as in Europe.

In 1967 at the Omo River in Ethiopia, more recent fossils of early man were found in sediments dated at some 130 000 years old. Amongst a collection of limb and jaw bones, two skulls were unearthed but the researchers who uncovered them were perplexed. They both had the same brain capacity, but the shape of the two skulls differed greatly, although they were found in sediments of the same age. The first, known not surprisingly as Omo I, resembled the skull of modern man. It had thinner bone and was rounded at the back and sides, although it did have a brow ridge like more primitive hominids. A lower jaw found alongside Omo I in-

DNA FILAMENT *A strand of DNA from the nucleus of a cell is the material that enables geneticists to track the evolution of our ancestors.*

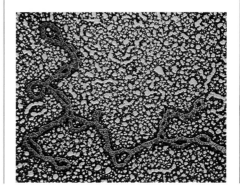

dicated a modern-shaped chin. Omo II, by contrast, had a thick-boned skull and an angular back to the cranium where strong neck muscles would have been attached. Both skulls evidently dated from the transition between *Homo erectus* and *Homo sapiens*, yet the variability in this local population was quite marked.

From this kind of evidence it becomes clearer how gradual the transition was. No single factor appears to have accelerated the change. Hunting techniques most probably improved and stone tools became more

THE FIRST CARPENTERS

Wood must have been important to our ancient ancestors during the Palaeolithic period and stone tools would probably have been used to fashion it. Microscopic examination of stone tools has revealed minute grooves indicating that some were used to shape wood. The tools have survived but the wood has not . . . or so the experts assumed until 1985, when Japanese palaeontologists found a board of mulberry wood (from a warm-climate tree now extinct in Japan but surviving in China and Korea) preserved in a waterlogged site. The board is about 11 in (28 cm) long and 2 in (5 cm) wide, and was probably shaped, flaked and even polished. It comes to a point at one end. It is estimated to be about 52 000 years old.

sophisticated, but no great cultural shift happened until thousands of years later, when modern *Homo sapiens* settled, cultivated crops and domesticated animals.

DOWN THE FEMALE LINE

While there is a dearth of fossil bones, some interesting evidence has come from the genetics laboratory. This is enough for scientists to put forward a plausible theory of the emergence of modern humans, based on information they have gained from a form of DNA (the substance responsible for transmitting genetic information from one generation to the next) known as mitochondrial DNA.

DNA is contained in both the nucleus of a cell and the mitochondria, specialised structures within the cell responsible for the chemical processes that cause the release of energy. Both kinds of DNA change, or mutate, very gradually over the generations, creating different lineages within a population, each with slightly different DNA structures. By studying these variations in different populations across the globe, scientists have found some fascinating clues to the early origins of mankind.

Essentially, since variations accumulate over time, the more variations there are, the older the population should be. Having established the rate at which the mutations leading to these variations generally occur, scientists can even give a rough estimate of when the population might have originated. In fact, of course, the picture is never as simple or revealing as that. For example, the rate of change in the DNA of the cell's nucleus is so slow – measured over hundreds of thousands of years – that it has little to tell us about the relatively recent origins of modern *Homo sapiens*. Mitochondrial DNA is far more useful in this respect.

Mitochondria contain many copies of one particular strand of DNA arranged in a circle – this has the advantage of being easier to read than the more complex nuclear DNA. Mitochondrial DNA also contains only the mother's DNA, unlike nuclear DNA which contains genetic material from both parents. This is because, when the sperm fertilises the egg, only the male nucleus passes into the egg, leaving the rest of the sperm, including its mitochondria, outside. Thus specific female lineages can be identified. Furthermore, mitochondrial DNA accumulates mutations about ten times faster than nuclear DNA, and therefore yields more information about the relatively recent past.

Early work using this approach was carried out at the University of California at Berkeley and at Stanford University. It demonstrated that modern Africans show the

MAMMOTH TASK *With a scarcity of trees on the Russian steppes, ancient man made huts from whatever was available, including mammoth bones.*

greatest degree of variability among human populations, suggesting Africa as the most probable site for modern man's origins. The scientists later established that all the female lineages, from across the globe, which are revealed by mitochondrial DNA can be traced to an unknown common ancestor who must have lived some 200 000 years ago in Africa. She was dubbed by the Press 'Mitochondrial Eve', but this name was misleading. Eve was

STONE-AGE SURGERY

Surgeons working with archaeologists from the University of Colorado in the USA have tested stone scalpels made from obsidian (volcanic glass). They discovered that the obsidian scalpels are sharper than, and superior to, steel and diamond blades, and considerably less expensive to produce. The replicas were modelled on blades that were manufactured by Maya Indians in Central America in 2000 BC.

an individual common ancestor but far from being an isolated female living with an isolated male as in the Genesis story, she was a member of a substantial population of archaic humans living in Africa at that time. Her female relatives, many of whom would also have been our ancestors, left no traces in the mitochondrial record simply because they had only sons or no offspring at all.

The interpretation of the mitochondrial

data has been controversial, at worst rejected as invalid, at best considered as one line of evidence that needs to be validated by others. At the same time, however, techniques for interpreting the data have been refined, leading to new findings. More recent research at Pennsylvania State University has suggested that modern humans arose somewhere in Africa about 135 000 years ago. This was followed, about 100 000 years ago, by an exodus out of Africa. Populations of modern man remained in Africa but several 'clans' headed north, south, east and west. According to this theory, some 15 clans of early modern humans reached Australia by about 50 000 years ago, 36 clans settled in Europe about 40 000 years ago and 31 clans headed for the northern parts of Asia, settling there about 20 000 years ago.

MORE EVIDENCE FROM AFRICA

An African origin for modern man is supported by evidence from Klasies River Mouth in South Africa where fossils have features, such as a rounded skull with a large brain and a strongly developed chin, that are unmistakably modern. The specimens are dated at 100 000 years old. Other South African fossils suggest the emergence of modern *Homo sapiens* in southern Africa, with populations migrating northwards, first to North Africa and the Middle East and eventually to Eurasia where they competed successfully with the archaic *Homo sapiens* populations and replaced them.

One very significant find comes from the south-west flank of Mount Qafzeh in Israel.

GETTING A LIKENESS One of the earliest human portraits was carved in limestone in a Cave near Vienne in the Rhone Valley about 13 000 years ago.

NEW BLADES *Cro-Magnon man used parallel-sided blades for woodworking and as spear-tips.*

Here, fossil skeletons, looking undoubtedly modern, have been found in simple graves in sediments dated at about 100 000 years old. These may indicate a northern African origin for modern man, followed by migrations both north and south. Unfortunately there are few fossils from this part of the world that can help to solve the mystery.

On the other hand, the discovery at Qafzeh, while posing a new question, does help to solve an old one – that of the status of the Neanderthals. With modern *Homo sapiens* living in the Middle East about 100 000 years ago there is no way in which the Neanderthals, living at the same time, could have been the direct ancestors of mankind. The two species overlapped for at least 70 000 years. The Neanderthals were most probably therefore an evolutionary sideline, rather than the ancestors of modern Europeans.

CRO-MAGNON MAN

About 40 000 years ago the transition from *erectus* to *sapiens* was complete and the archaic forms of *Homo sapiens* had finally given way to modern man. Populations of modern *Homo sapiens* were established in

Africa and Eurasia, were entering Australasia and about to enter the Americas. The period is known in archaeology as the Upper Palaeolithic.

The first significant fossil from this period in man's prehistory was found in Europe. In 1868 railway workers at Les Eyzies in the Dordogne region of France uncovered the first recognised fossil of modern man, near the Hotel Cro-Magnon. The Old Man of Cro-Magnon, one of five skeletons that had been buried in a shallow rock shelter, had a high forehead and greatly reduced brow ridges like modern human beings. A small section of skull and part of

the face had been eaten away. It was thought that the old man suffered from actinomycosis, a devastating disease caused by a mysterious fungal infection.

The fossils showed modern people to be relatively tall, slightly built and long-limbed. Females stood some 5 ft 6 in (1.7 m) tall and weighed 120 lb (55 kg); the males were about 6 ft (1.8 m) tall and weighed 155 lb (70 kg). This size and shape are best suited to tropical, subtropical and warm temperate climates, further evidence perhaps that modern man originated in Africa. The skull had a rounded brain case, high forehead and small face. Brain capacity was about

85 cu in (1400 cm³) for a mature adult. To all intents and purposes, humans of this period would have resembled people today and would not have stood out, if dressed appropriately, in a city street.

Cro-Magnon people lived in rock shelters in western Europe or specially built huts on the steppes of eastern Europe. Their living sites are littered with a characteristic tool or weapon, the parallel-sided blade. Some blades, it is thought, were used to work wood and bone, while others were attached to wooden handles and used as spears and harpoons. There is evidence that animals were either trapped in leather snares or driven

THE BOOMERANG: KILLING BY THROWING

A boomerang made from a mammoth's tusk was found in 1987 in a cave beside a river gorge in southern Poland. The carved and polished weapon was 2½ ft (76 cm) long, more than 2 in (5 cm) wide and about ½ in (1.3 cm) thick. It was probably 23 000 years old, which makes it the world's oldest boomerang. Animal remains in the Polish cave indicate that it was inhabited by a group of ancient migrant hunters who killed mainly reindeer using the boomerang. These fossils also indicate that

Europe was undergoing a cold climatic phase at the time.

Boomerangs and kylies (killing sticks that, unlike boomerangs, do not return) are not exclusively Australian. They have been found in Africa with an estimated age of 9000 years. Boomerangs were common in Egyptian tombs, and some with gold caps at each end were found in the 14th century BC tomb of Tutankhamun.

In Europe an oak boomerang, dated about 3000 BC, was found in 1962 in coastal sand dunes near Velsen in Holland. An even older specimen dated 5000 BC was unearthed at Braband, Jutland. In fact, boomerangs have been used by peoples all over the world. Hopi

Indians, Inuit (Eskimos), Polynesians and Indians also had boomerangs. Several wooden specimens have been found at Wyrie Swamp in Australia dated at 10 000-9000 years old. They are accurate over distances of up to 220 yd (200 m), much farther than a person could throw a stone or spear. Modern replicas of many of the ancient finds

have proved that the weapons actually do work. Copies of the Dutch and Egyptian boomerangs revealed impressive flight paths with a sharp turn at the end, thus returning the weapon to the thrower. Boomerangs were used by ancient peoples in many parts of the world for thousands of years until the bow and arrow took over.

RETURN OF THE BOOMERANG
Each specimen in the collection of ancient boomerangs (right) has the same aerodynamic properties – enabling it to be thrown over long distances and bringing it back to the thrower – as a modern-day boomerang used by the Aborigines of Australia (left).

into pit traps before they were killed. Cave paintings in the innermost, less accessible parts of caves indicate a view of things that goes beyond the purely practical or even decorative and shows that Cro-Magnon had developed a notion of symbolism. Elaborate burial sites tell the same story of a concern for the symbolic. They also had a taste for personal adornment, making bracelets and necklaces. From this point onwards in prehistory humans can be recognised and categorised as much by the products of their culture as by their anatomy and physiology.

Elsewhere in the world, other sites show-

ANCIENT MURALS *The rock art of Lascaux includes this horse, known as the 'Chinese horse', crossing the roof. The brown lines could be hunters' spears.*

ing the emergence of modern man have been found. At first the Far East was the focus of study. Java and Wadjak in modern Indonesia were the centre of attention in 1889 and 1890 respectively. Early human remains, indicating a possible route for man's invasion of Australia, had attracted the Dutch doctor and palaeontologist Eugène Dubois to the region – he later discovered the fossils of the *Homo erectus* known as Java man. In China, the upper cave at Zhoukoudian has revealed skulls of people looking like the Cro-Magnons of Europe. Accompanying them are stone and bone tools, ornaments and red ochre in sediments which date to 25 000 years ago. In Malaysia, at the Niah Cave in Sarawak, pieces of a skull and foot bones, dated to at least 40 000 years ago, were found in 1958.

In South Africa, modern *Homo sapiens*

fossils perhaps as much as 80 000 years old have been discovered at Border Cave, KwaZulu. Similar specimens from Fish Hoek, also in South Africa, were dated at 36 000 years old. Modern man had spread throughout southern Africa. Evidence is also accumulating about his spread into the New World.

In fact, modern man was settling in most parts of the world, in a range of climates and conditions. During the ensuing tens of thousands of years, the climate also changed, becoming colder. It stimulated humans to design and wear more sophisticated clothes and build effective shelters. Man was able to adapt, not so much through anatomical and physiological changes, but more by a cultural evolution, using ingenuity and rapidly developing technology.

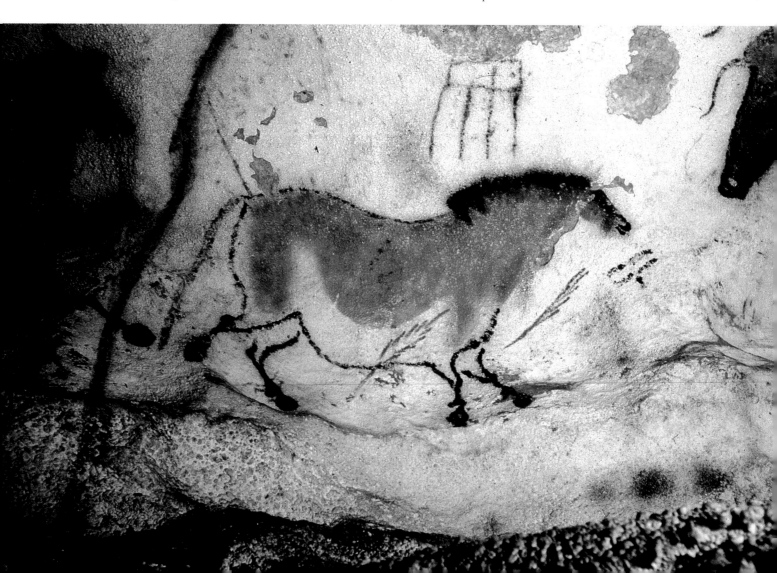

MIGRATION AND 2 TRAVEL

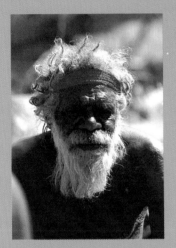

LINEAGE *Australian Aborigines are descended from people who crossed the sea from Asia.*

ALTHOUGH DEBATE CONTINUES ABOUT THE EXACT COURSE OF HUMAN EVOLUTION, ONE FACT IS NOT DISPUTED: FROM THE VERY BEGINNING, MODERN HUMANS WERE ON THE MOVE, SEARCHING OUT THE BEST PLACES TO LIVE, TO HUNT AND TO FORAGE. NOWHERE IN THE WORLD WAS BEYOND HUMANKIND'S REACH. NEITHER MOUNTAINS, NOR OCEANS, NOR DESERTS, NOR JUNGLES POSED A BARRIER. WITH A LARGE BRAIN AND AN INTELLIGENT, INNOVATIVE MIND, MODERN PEOPLE WERE ABLE TO TRAVEL THROUGH AND SETTLE IN ANY ENVIRONMENT, AND IN DOING SO, GROUPS DEVELOPED PHYSICAL ADAPTATIONS AND SOCIAL PATTERNS THAT ENABLED THEM TO SURVIVE NEW, SOMETIMES HOSTILE, TERRAIN AND CLIMATIC CONDITIONS.

EARLY ART *Rock paintings in Canada prove man's wanderlust.*

OUT OF AFRICA?
OR ASIA?

Modern humans either emerged from Africa, or sprang up simultaneously in Africa and Asia. Whichever way they travelled, they evolved into groups that were well adapted to too much sun, too much snow, or to just a little of both.

Most experts believe that mankind evolved in Africa. Conditions there were right for a remarkable evolutionary push that saw a large-brained ape start to fill ecological niches denied to other creatures because they lacked its brain power. The brainy ones did not stay in Africa for long, however. From the earliest times, modern man and his forebears were inquisitive, not only about their immediate environment, but also about what lay around the next bend or over the next hill. They began to explore, moving from one place to another in search of safer sites to live in and better sources of food to gather, scavenge or hunt.

Africa's Great Rift Valley, where some of mankind's early activities were focused, was a geologically violent place. Volcanoes and earthquakes dominated the lives of plants and animals. Periodically, thick layers of volcanic ash enveloped the land, burying the primary foodstuff, green plants. There must have been considerable

pressure on any animal with the wherewithal – a large brain, tools and a society that encouraged cooperation – to seek out a better life elsewhere. This is precisely what early people did.

The story as it has long been told by most experts is that, between 2 million and 1 million years ago, *Homo erectus*, the predecessor of early modern man, started to spread out from Africa to colonise the entire Old World. The next exodus, according to this view, took place about 100 000 years ago, when straggling bands of early modern man, *Homo sapiens* himself, walked out of Africa and took over the world, replacing the descendants of the earlier migration. Their first move was into the Middle East, then into the Far East about 60 000 years ago, and Europe 35 000 years ago.

An alternative theory, however, proposes that man-like creatures (hominids) expanded their populations into the world outside Africa at a much earlier date, maybe 2 million years ago. Modern man then evolved gradually from more ancient 'versions' of himself in several different parts of the world – East Africa, Asia Minor, northern China and Indonesia.

So far, there is no universally agreed answer to the controversy, but studies of DNA show that there is only a 0.1 per cent variation in all human DNA, supporting a relatively recent, 'one-stop' origin, probably in Africa about 100 000 years ago. If evolution had taken place gradually from different sources in the very distant past, the DNA from the different races would by now vary a great deal – but it does not. No matter which race we belong to – Inuit (Eskimos), Pygmies, Aborigines, Celts – humans are all genetically almost identical. Mankind has not had time to diverge in its biological makeup in any significant way.

Different races rarely have unique features, for they share most of their genes. But when particular genes appear more fre-

SEA OF GALILEE Looking much as it did tens of thousands of years ago, this region in the Middle East was the crossroads of migrating modern man.

HUMAN MIGRATION Setting out, probably from Africa, modern humans distributed themselves rapidly to all parts of the world.

quently in a population, they will inevitably emphasise certain features. The influence driving this appears to be environmental. Inuit and other peoples of the far north tend to be short, stocky and powerfully built, an adaptation to the cold. They have less surface area from which heat can escape. Negroid, southern Asian and Australian Aboriginal peoples have skin pigmentation that protects them against harmful ultraviolet rays from the sun. It is a shield that northern races, plunged into darkness for much of the year, do not need.

The reasons that races exist at all are probably the same ones that explain differences in other animal populations. First, the distribution of particular genes among humans will inevitably be uneven, simply by chance. Secondly, those living at the centre of an area inhabited by a particular group will become more isolated from other groups and therefore more specialised than those at the boundaries, except where the boundary areas are isolated. The specialisation of those inhabiting the 'interior' enables them to live in that place. Those living on the edges are more likely to interbreed with neighbouring populations, so patterns formed by their genes will be mixed.

ANCIENT MAN IN ASIA

Although Africa is still regarded as the most probable birthplace of mankind, our understanding of the actual timing of the exodus into Europe and Asia changes with every new fossil find. In November 1995, for ex-

ample, the palaeoanthropological world was rocked by an announcement from a site in China. A few years earlier, in 1988, a fossil jaw had been found in the Longgupo Cave, near the Chang Jiang (Yangtze) River in south-central China. At the time it was thought to be from *Homo erectus*, but a more recent examination by researchers from China, Canada and the USA was now suggesting that it came from an even earlier fossil hominid. It was most probably *Homo habilis* or the closely related *Homo ergaster*, hitherto known only from Africa, dated 2 million years ago.

One theory is that hominid evolution started in Africa some 5 million years ago with an australopithecine that has yet to be identified. The argument continues that the *Homo* lineage evolved with large-brained *Homo habilis* in Africa about 2.5 million years ago. The even larger-brained *Homo erectus* evolved about 2 million years ago, again in Africa, and ranged far and wide on the first migration out of Africa. In short, it was thought that most of the major events in our prehistory had their origins in Africa. The new interpretation of the Longgupo fossil puts all this in doubt.

Some researchers have poured scorn on the claim. A few believe that the fossil jaw came from a fossil ape, not a human, and others suggest that the fossil – part of a jaw-bone with a premolar and a molar tooth and an isolated upper incisor – provides insufficient evidence for an accurate identification. The premolar, however, has both the crown and the root, which provide important clues. The root, in particular, is a double root of a kind associated with *Homo ergaster*. It is more primitive than the single root found in *Homo erectus* and modern humans.

Other finds in the area confirm that fossil hominids were present in the south-east corner of Asia more than 1.8 million years ago. Two fossils from Java, dated 1.6 and 1.8 million years ago, are clearly *Homo erectus*. Although they could have been descendants of migrants from Africa, the new information suggests that *Homo erectus* might have evolved, not in Africa, but in Asia, and that the Java fossils might be from an ancient Asian stock.

This would suggest that a population of *Homo ergaster* or *Homo habilis* left Africa earlier than we had imagined, and that *Homo erectus* evolved from them in Asia,

LIFE OF A CAVE When the Zhoukoudian cave developed an opening to the outside, people moved in. Roof collapse and sedimentary build-up slowly filled the cave and occupants at different times lived in different parts, until they eventually had to move out. Left behind was the debris, buried in layers, of 200 000 years of human habitation.

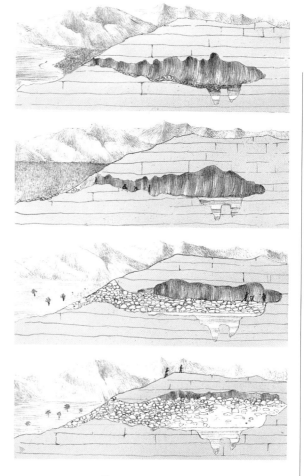

spreading back into Europe and Africa. Hominid remains and stone tools, which may be as much as 1.6 million years old, have been unearthed at Dmanisi in Georgia and suggest that *Homo erectus* was poised to enter Europe at about the same time that the Longgupo fossil was alive. Where it was travelling from, the south-east or the south-west, is still unclear.

An earlier report, from 1987, supports the notion that *Homo habilis* or one of his relatives was the first intercontinental

ASIAN ANCESTOR Peking Man, an Asian form of Homo erectus, *was found at the Chinese cave site at Zhoukoudian (formerly Choukoutien).*

traveller. The evidence came from the British Archaeological Mission to Pakistan in the form of several 2-million-year-old stone tools discovered during an excavation near Rawalpindi. The outcrop in which they were found is the head of a small waterfall in the wet season, and gradual erosion had exposed the artefacts.

Claims like these for an Asian origin for modern humans have been made from time to time in the past, but the dating of the material has always been suspect. It is particularly difficult to date a bone or artefact found sitting on top of a deposit rather than embedded in an identifiable stratum of rock or sediment. The Rawalpindi finds, according to a team from the University of Sheffield who helped to find them, were firmly embedded in a deposit of gritstone and conglomerate – sedimentary rock consisting of large fragments mixed in with

ASIAN THRESHOLD The evidence for the presence of early man in Asia was found through this limestone cave entrance at Zhoukoudian.

finer material – and had to be chiselled out. The deposit was at least 2 million years old because of its position in sedimentary rocks known to have been forced upwards by movements in the Earth's crust 2.1 to 1.9 million years ago. A layer of ash above the layer with the stone tools is firmly dated at 1.6 million years old, and the stone-tool layer itself is thought to be at least 300 000 years older.

Another problem with stone artefacts is that they may be the natural product of, say, river erosion. Pebbles pushed along on the bed of a river often crack to create a stone that resembles a stone tool. The Rawalpindi stones, however, appear to be man-made. One piece, composed of quartzite, has been struck in three directions by a hammerstone and has seven flakes taken from it. The multifaceted flaking, together with the 'fresh' appearance of the scar, indicates that early hominids must have made the tool. Which

hominids they were is the subject of further research, but the find is another piece of evidence suggesting that we may have to re-think the timing of early man's first forays out of Africa. The savannah of northern Pakistan and India might have played host to events similar to those taking place in eastern and southern Africa.

DENTAL RECORDS

Further evidence for an Asian origin for man comes from dental research. In a worldwide study of teeth, particularly of their roots and cusps, researchers at Arizona State University examined those of 12 000 individuals from 83 locations around the globe. Archaeological material dominated the survey, but modern teeth were also included. The research took 20 years to complete and the results, reported in 1989, were predictably controversial.

Certain traits, such as the number and

types of teeth, vary very little among groups of humans all across the world, but others provide a new window on the history and movements of different populations. These traits, notably the form of the cusps and the roots, differ from group to group but are stable within a group over time. They are generally unaffected by environmental factors such as climate, and are most probably shaped by random changes as small groups expand into new territories.

Study of the cusps and roots showed that Australian Aborigines are more closely related to Africans than they are to their Melanesian neighbours. Polynesian and Mi-

CAVE OF ZHOUKOUDIAN
Professor Woo Ju-Kang, one of today's authorities on Homo erectus *remains in Asia, surveys the Zhoukoudian excavation site.*

cronesian samples showed a closer affinity to those of South-east Asia. Overall, two major clusters were found: a group in north-east Asia which split off from the rest and eventually crossed the Bering land bridge to become the Amerindians, and a group representing the rest of the human family – including Europeans, Africans, South-east Asians and native Australians. Dental examination can also suggest which was the ancestral group; it would be the one with the fewest specialised features that also matched most closely the 'average' dental signature of all the rest. This turned out to be the group from South-east Asia. This work, however, has been challenged by scientists at the Natural History Museum in London, who regard the teeth of Africans and Australians as closer to the ancestral pattern.

Another argument turns to the fossil record. According to an American scientist, an examination of Asian fossil hominids shows that the more recent Asians in the fossil record evolved from the more ancient ones, whereas according to the 'Out of Africa' theory the ancestors of modern humans would have replaced all earlier populations, despite the fact that these earlier populations had continuously adapted to conditions in various regions of the Old World for about a million years. This scientist believes that it is stretching credibility to accept that the forerunner of modern man, which had adapted to the tropics at one extreme and icy-cold climates at the other, should become extinct without trace.

The fossil evidence for the Asian origins of modern man includes two 350 000-year-old skulls found near the Han River in Yunxian, China. The skulls had squashed faces, like those of modern humans. They were originally classified as *Homo erectus*, however, because many other features were primitive, such as a long, low brain case. On the other hand, the facial structure was more like that of *Homo sapiens*. It prompted scientists from the Hubei Institute of Archaeology and the University of California at Berkeley to suggest that these ancient hominids could have been the ancestors, or closely related to the ancestors, of modern humans.

Much is still not known. Although DNA research seems to favour the 'Out of Africa' theory, some geneticists have questioned the interpretations drawn from it, while other researchers still prefer to plot mankind's evolution from the fossil record, which as yet is far from complete.

ORIGIN OF RACES

Scientists at Oxford University in Britain, working with doctors from all over the world, have been mapping part of one of the human chromosomes. The task includes analysing the structure of chromosome 11 in the region of the 'betaglobin gene cluster' – this programmes the building code for certain key proteins. During their researches, the scientists found several sequences of DNA that are known as 'polymorphisms'. These parts of the chromosome do not themselves programme the code for any proteins but form part of the intervening sequences between genes. They are 'filler' sequences, and they mutate, or change, faster than regions that provide the code for a specific function.

They examined the same region on the chromosomes of 600 people from eight racial groups in different parts of the world – from Britain, Cyprus, Italy, India, Thailand, Melanesia, Polynesia and Africa. The first discovery was that modern races living close geographically have very similar patterns of polymorphisms. African and non-African races, however, differ substantially. Only 5 per cent of the sub-Saharan Africans tested, for example, had the same polymorphisms as all the European races.

The scientists concluded that the non-African races never had, or have lost, the ancient polymorphisms of the sub-Saharan peoples. They also suggested that the founder group that left Africa to migrate into other continents was relatively small, being a sub-group of the 5 per cent, and that the whole world population outside Africa – Asians, Americans, Polynesians and Europeans – is descended from a group of maybe just 1000 individuals who set out from Africa between 100 000 and 50 000 years ago.

ADAPTATIONS *The Inuit hunter from the Canadian Arctic is stockily built to conserve heat, whereas the Andalucian (right) has lungs and a blood system adapted for mountain living.*

LIFE IN THE SUN *The people of the Pokot tribe in Kenya are well adapted to cope with the sun, heat and dust of life on the hot savannah.*

THE FIRST AMERICANS

The date when the first humans crossed from Asia to North America over the Bering land bridge is the subject of much debate. Moving south as and when the ice caps allowed, they found a continent that was teeming with animal life.

The first Americans almost certainly came from Asia. Dental studies show that southern China was the boundary between two distinct groups. In South-east Asia, the aboriginal peoples of modern Thailand, Burma, Cambodia, Laos, Malaysia, Taiwan, Borneo, Indonesia and the Philippines formed one group, while to the north the Chinese, Mongols, Japanese and peoples such as the Buryats of eastern Siberia formed the other. The northern, mongoloid group probably evolved in what is now China and then spread through the rest of north-eastern Asia, where they hunt-

ed bison, reindeer and mammoth and fished for salmon. Some members of this group are believed to have crossed into North America.

Excavations in the eastern part of Siberia have unearthed evidence that such people did indeed live there about 35 000 years ago. It includes burial pits and artefacts such as stone tools and decorative beads. The makers of these objects lived in shelters, the re-

mains of which suggest that they were tents or wigwams made from animal skins. Each tent probably contained several families, all of whom had their own hearths, for several hearths are evident in every shelter.

The northern peoples did not stop when they reached Siberia's north-eastern tip, the Chukchi Peninsula, and the Bering Strait that separates it from Alaska. Several times in the recent past Asia and the Americas have been joined by a land bridge, dubbed Beringia by modern experts. However, when and exactly how these early groups made the crossing, as with all aspects of mankind's emergence, is a matter of considerable debate. The current thinking is that there was more than one passage.

One theory has it that three successive parties left northeast Asia at different times and crossed into Alaska. Thence they made their way into the rest of the Americas. Studies of teeth, genetics and native languages have been combined to paint the picture. According to this, the first group to arrive gave rise to all the South American Indians and most of the North American Indians. They were primarily hunters of land mammals. The second wave

FORBIDDING LANDSCAPE
Tundra, pockmarked by frozen ponds, was the landscape that greeted the first Americans migrating from Asia.

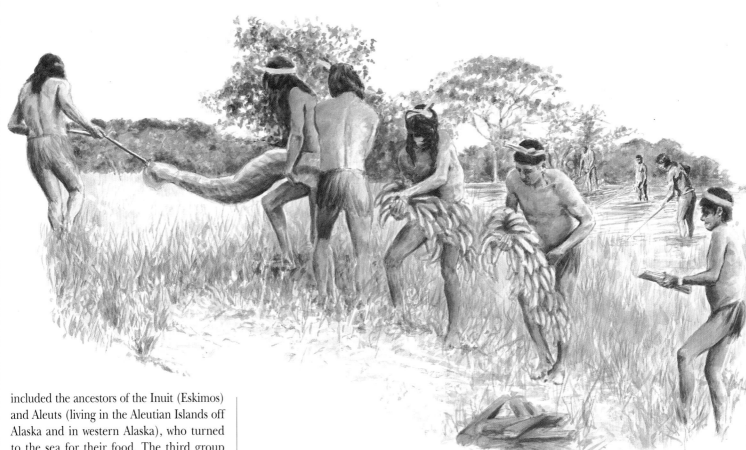

included the ancestors of the Inuit (Eskimos) and Aleuts (living in the Aleutian Islands off Alaska and in western Alaska), who turned to the sea for their food. The third group gave rise to the Navaho and Apache tribes, along with Alaskan and British Columbian Indians, all of whom speak a language known as Na-Dene.

THE CLOVIS SCENARIO

Human populations spread very rapidly, and the first Americans were no exception. They may have arrived on the American continent as recently as 12 000 years ago, and had reached the southern tip of South America within 2000 years . . . or had they? The traditional view is known as the Clovis scenario, after an important find at Clovis, New Mexico, of fluted stone blades believed to be 11 000 years old. It maintains that populations of big-game hunters migrated from Asia across the land bridge of Beringia during the waning years of the Ice Age about 12 000 years ago. But more recent finds have called into question whether this was the first invasion of the New World. People may have made it to the Americas long before

this, although it must be said that all the very early evidence from both the North and South American sites is still subject to hot debate.

In 1973 students from the University of Pittsburgh found artefacts and pieces of charcoal at Meadowcroft, a cave site at Cross Creek in south-western Pennsylvania. The cave had been occupied by successive generations of early Americans who left behind pottery, tools and remains of food – snail shells, nuts, seeds and the bones of turkey, deer and elk – as well as the first signs of agriculture in the shape of squash and corn remains. But the surprise for the researchers came with the dating of the older deposits.

At one stage in its history the cave's roof collapsed, separating two periods of occupation in the deposits. The younger period is between 13 000 and 11 000 years old, the older one between 19 000 and 12 800 years. Stone tools, including knives, small blades and spear tips, together with the hammer

CHILEAN VILLAGE *A pre-Ice Age village in a peat bog at Monte Verde suggests man migrated from the Old World earlier than was first thought. Overleaf: When the first Americans reached the plains they found meat, in the form of bison, in plentiful supply. They chased them into ditches or ravines, where they could kill them.*

tools with which they were manufactured, were all there, but the oldest artefact was a fragment of basketry. It consists of a 2 x 3 in (50 x 75 mm) portion of bark-like material, most probably part of a plaited basket or mat. Scientists using radiocarbon dating have estimated that it is 19 600 years old, which means that the site was occupied by *continued on page 80*

MEADOWCROFT, USA
The excavations are revealing that the first Americans reached Pennsylvania by about 20 000 years ago.

such as jaguar, deer, pigs, lizards, armadillos, flightless rheas and freshwater crabs.

When excavations were started by scientists from France and Brazil in 1978, stone tools were found on the cave floor alongside circular stone hearths and food-storage pits. Charcoal in the hearths was radiocarbon dated and estimated to be between 32 000 and 17 000 years old.

In sites nearby, the remains of the local animals have been found – giant sloths, horses, peccaries, large camels, early llamas and giant armadillos. All were pursued by early human hunters who lived many thousands of years before the end of the last Ice Age. How, then, did the people who occupied these sites reach the Americas?

INTERGLACIAL CROSSINGS

During the Ice Age, lasting from 1.6 million to around 10 000 years ago, glaciers periodically covered large portions of the Northern Hemisphere and the climate and

early man before the end of the Ice Age. Some specialists, however, suggest that the samples may have been contaminated by the presence of small coal particles in the deposits, making the dates come out older than they really are.

STONE TOOLS IN A PEAT BOG

There are other examples of early human activity all over the Americas. Stone tools, the remains of a hut of crudely cut logs and other signs of a camp occupied 13 000 years ago have been found in a peat bog at Monte Verde in Chile. Stone and wooden tools (including digging sticks and lances), the bones of llamas and mastodons, together with pieces of charcoal, have been dated to 15 000 and maybe 19 000 years ago.

Other sites suggested by some experts as being pre-Clovis include Bluefish Caves in Canada's Yukon Territory, where claims have been made for 25 000-year-old bones, and Taima-taima in Venezuela, which has yielded a butchered mastodon bone that may be 13 000 years old. Yet another example is the Orogrande Cave in New Mexico, where a clay hearth with what may be a

28 000-year-old human palm print, is accompanied by stone tools thought by some to be 29 000 years old. An ancient site in Brazil is even more spectacular and certainly more controversial. It is a sandstone rock shelter, 230 ft (70 m) long, at Pedra Furada (or Toca do Boqueirao do Sitio da Pedra Furada to give the cave its full name).

The shelter is one of 260 found among spectacular scenery where 800 ft (240 m) cliffs extend for about 120 miles (193 km) between a flat plain to one side and jagged mountains to the other. All but 20 of the shelters have astonishing displays of rock art, painted in red and yellow ochre together with other colours – black, white and grey. They depict abstract symbols, trees, stick-like cartoon people, and animals

CLOVIS POINTS *Fluted stone blades are characteristic of the Clovis people, who were once thought to be the first Americans.*

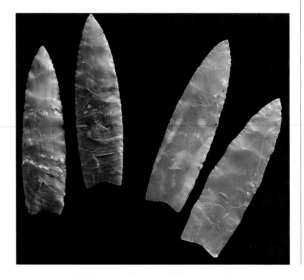

THE EXTERMINATORS

When the first Americans arrived in the New World, they found it teeming with big mammals that are now extinct: seven types of elephant-like mammoths and mastodons, ground sloths weighing 3 tons, armadillo-like glyptodons, bear-sized beavers and various sabre-toothed cats. It has long been assumed that the humans exterminated these large mammals in what is thought to have been the most concentrated extinction of big animals since the demise of the dinosaurs 65 million years ago. But other possibilities exist in what is another area of puzzling controversy.

Alternative theories hold, for example, that a fluctuating climate accounted for the extinctions. Abrupt and violent changes in temperature and precipitation patterns would have had a considerable effect on the vegetation on which these large herbivores depended and could have led to their demise.

A compromise position suggests that man and climate were in collusion. The changing climate resulted in fewer ecological niches available for large mammals. Their populations were gradually concentrated into smaller areas, where they were more vulnerable to predators.

These early human invaders had the weaponry to annihilate the North American 'megafauna'. They had spears and stone projectiles, and they had the sheer weight of numbers. Ignoring the pre-Clovis debate, if a party of 30 or so hunters had pushed south more than 11 000 years ago, in just 300 years their ranks could have swollen to 300 000.

According to one expert, they could have migrated at an average rate of about 10 miles (16 km) a year and doubled their number at each generation. On this estimate, they could have accounted for about 100 million large mammals on the way.

LARGE MAMMALS *Mammoths, bison and caribou were all slaughtered by the first Americans using effective weapons, such as stone-tipped spears launched from wooden spear-throwers (known as the* atlatl *by the Aztecs of South America). The design of the spear points was altered according to the prey being sought. Large, sharp Clovis points were used for mammoth; the smaller, sharply pointed Folsom points for bison; and Hi Lo points for caribou. Concentrations of different points have been found at different sites.*

- Caribou
- Bison
- Mammoth
- Hi Lo distribution
- Clovis distribution
- Folsom distribution
- ▲ Folsom sites
- ■ Hi Lo sites
- ● Clovis sites

sea level fluctuated with the coming and going of the ice. But the ice sheets were never a permanent feature in most parts of the Western Hemisphere.

Interglacial periods occurred from around 60 000 to 25 000 years ago, when the climate in the Northern Hemisphere became milder than during the periods before and after it. In the Old World, and in Europe in particular, there was intense human activity. *Homo sapiens* was replacing *Homo neanderthalensis*, and stone-blade tool-kits and cave paintings were appearing. Modern man was migrating into Japan and Australia and had reached the eastern part of Siberia. He was poised to invade the Americas. There was, however, one obstacle. By the time the climate had warmed up the sea level had risen between 30 and 60 ft (9 and 18 m) due to melting ice, and the land bridge to North America was no longer continuous. Potential invaders would have been confronted with a strait about 12 miles (19 km) wide, with free water in summer and solid ice in winter.

There was plenty to tempt them across, however, as there was an abundance of food

HUNTING PARTY *Examples of early American art are provided by the Cueva Pintada rock paintings at Baja California, Mexico.*

of the subsequent glacial period, when the land bridge had fully re-emerged. This migration then split into three groups when it reached the New World.

Another argument for pre-Clovis Americans comes from linguistics. A period of 12 000 years is considered too short for the various Native American languages to have developed in all their diversity. According to this argument, one migrant group speaking a single language must have arrived at least 60 000 years ago – before the ice melted and sea levels rose during the interglacial period – to reach the diversity that exists today. Alternatively, three groups of migrants, each speaking a different language, could have arrived 40 000 to 30 000 years ago, possibly using some kind of watercraft to cross the stretch of sea that had by then drowned the Bering land bridge.

If pre-Clovis Americans did make it across the Bering Strait during the interglacial period, their progress south and east would have been along well-defined ice-free routes. Some might have headed directly south into modern British Columbia. Here the climate and vegetation of valleys and lowlands would have been much the same as they are today, albeit a little cooler and drier. Farther east, the ice would have receded from much of the rest of present-day Canada, except for an ice sheet that remained around the Hudson Bay area.

As they penetrated farther into the continent, the bands of invaders would have encountered a variety of habitats – tundra, forests and swamps. With the steppe-tundra so rich in game, however, there would have been little temptation to try their luck in the great northern forests.

THE RETURN OF THE ICE AGE

Between 30 000 and 25 000 years ago, all this activity would have been radically altered, for the ice sheets returned. On the one hand, these locked up so much water as ice

on both sides of the strait. The vegetation, mostly grasses and herbs, would be described today as steppe-tundra, and it supported mammoths, giant bison and horses. (All of these later became extinct. It was the Spanish conquistadores arriving in the 16th century AD who reintroduced the horse into the Americas.)

In the light of the possible pre-Clovis finds, the three-wave theory has been modified, with some experts now suggesting that an earlier migration took place between 30 000 and 15 000 years ago – that is, at some time between the closing millennia of the interglacial period, when sea levels were dropping again, and the height that the sea fell to about 280 ft (85 m) below its present level, exposing the land bridge between Asia and Alaska. On the other hand, the rapid glaciation of the interior blocked many inland routes and forced people back into coastal regions such as Beringia – where conditions were less severe due to the influence of the sea.

Conditions in Beringia were not good for people, however, as the vegetation consisted of dwarf shrubs and bare tundra, much like today's high Arctic regions. Much more attractive was a broad area of continental shelf, very much less rugged than today's Pacific coast, that was exposed by the falling sea levels. Nomads might therefore have crossed the land bridge and then been drawn south along this coastal shelf. However, this ice-free corridor became blocked between 18 000 and 11 000 years ago.

By building small, primitive boats they could have carried on farther and farther south along the Pacific seaboard of North America and lived well in the process. The north-western Pacific Ocean was not covered with ice at that time – only coastal bays were. A wealth of seasonally nesting sea birds, mussel and clam beds, walrus, whales and seals would all have provided food. This is conjecture, however, since there is no evidence that any of it actually happened; what was then coast is now under many fathoms of water and difficult to study.

At the same time there is evidence that the glaciers did not cover the entire Northern Hemisphere, leaving more hospitable regions between the ice sheets. One such region existed between the great ice sheet that covered the centre of the continent and the glaciers of the mountainous north-west. It provided an ice-free corridor along which people could have moved south to escape the advancing ice. It follows the route

SAILING SOUTH *Early Americans may have used small boats made from skins stretched over a bone frame, propelled by paddles, to travel down the west coast of North America when the land routes were blocked by ice (right).*

of the eastern leg of the present-day Pacific flyway for migrating birds, and it is likely that 20 000 years ago there were already birds nesting along the route. They would have provided food for early pioneers, as well as musk oxen and small mammals such as voles.

By 11 000 years ago, the ice sheets had receded sufficiently for people to strike inland again. Equally, the melting ice meant that the sea level rose, so that the land bridge was drowned once more, preventing further migrations.

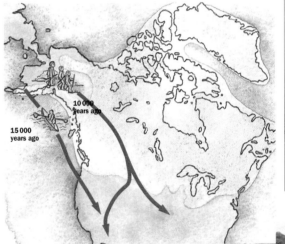

15 000 years ago

10 000 years ago

HONOURING THE DEAD

Nine thousand years ago, more than 3000 years before ancient Egypt emerged as a great civilisation, fishing folk living along the Pacific coast of what is now northern Chile and southern Peru were already making mummies of their dead. Living off the riches of the sea, they made their homes in the narrow, relatively fertile strip that fringes the ocean and in valleys carved by rivers flowing down from the Andes looming high on the eastern horizon. Between them and the mountains spread the Atacama Desert, the driest place on Earth. They lived in small communities, probably of between 10 and 50 people each, and had only the simplest of technology – stone knives, nets made of reeds, fish-hooks made from cactus spines or bone. Yet, by around 5000 BC, they were creating astonishingly sophisticated mummies, the first people known to have done so. They are referred to as the Chinchorro people because the first mummies found by modern archaeologists were discovered near a beach called Chinchorro.

The mummies are what make the Chinchorros especially interesting to students of

prehistory. They survived as a distinctive culture for nearly 6000 years, from around 7020 to 1100 BC, and throughout these millennia they preserved their dead. Moreover, unlike the ancient Egyptians, they did not simply preserve the bodies of nobles and kings – their small egalitarian communities did not boast such positions – but everybody: adult women and men, children, even the foetuses of mothers who had miscarried. At first they relied on the natural aridity of their environment; the intense dryness of the desert, combined with its abundant salt content, automatically desiccates and preserves bodies buried or left out in it. By around 5050 BC, however, they had learnt to assist nature, using man-devised methods to make their mummies. These techniques reached a peak of sophistication during the 2000-odd years between 4980 and 2800 BC, and then – for reasons that experts have not yet fathomed – declined until, by 1720 BC, the Chinchorros had reverted to allowing nature to do their mummification for them.

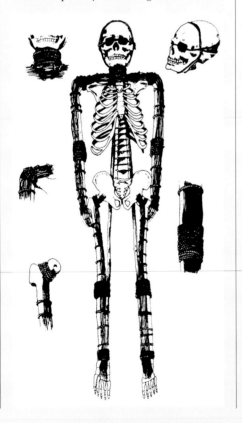

REBUILDING *The skeleton of a black mummy, the most elaborate of all the Chinchorro styles, was carefully stiffened using sticks and cords. The skull was sliced through to extract the brains.*

FAMILY IN THE SAND *These figures, discovered in the early 1980s, lie in the extended position characteristic of Chinchorro mummies. They were often buried in groups, which may have corresponded to the families they belonged to while alive.*

The Chinchorros had no form of writing, so all we know about them has to be deduced from the mummies themselves and other archaeological finds. None the less, archaeologists such as Bernardo Arriaza of the University of Nevada, Las Vegas, have managed to unravel many of their techniques. Essentially, during the peak period of the so-called 'black' mummies, these seem to have involved pulling the body apart, and then methodically reconstructing it. First, the head, hands and feet were removed, probably using stone knives made of quartz. Then the skin was peeled off. The brains were removed from the skull, the muscles and other soft tissue from the rest of the body, leaving a bare skeleton. This was then dried, using hot ashes – some bones have burn marks.

The skeleton was reinforced, using sticks bound onto the bones with cords made of animal skin or reed. Sticks were also used to

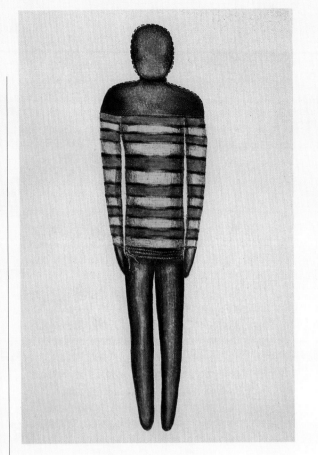

the work of specialists, who may have travelled from community to community as the need arose, and would have taken many days or weeks to complete – an astonishing investment of time and energy for people whose subsistence, though viable, was rarely ample.

Why did they do it? Clearly, these mummies were of vital importance to communities. The evidence is that the mummies were not finally buried until a long time – possibly many years – after the death of the individual. With their reinforced skeletons, they were easily portable on reed mats. Experts such as Arriaza believe that they played a central role in community celebrations. The process of mummification itself would almost certainly have been accompanied by

wake-like festivities. Then, whenever any community rites and festivals took place – such as annual fertility rites or initiation ceremonies for young adults – the mummies would have been carried to the scene and duly honoured, possibly with ritual gifts of food. Customs like these were features of many later Andean cultures.

For the Chinchorro people, as for many later Andeans, the worlds of the living and the dead – and for the Chinchorros that meant all of the dead, including unborn foetuses – were parts of a seamless whole. The dead were probably seen as being in close contact with the spiritual powers believed to control the vagaries of climate and such terrors as earthquakes and tidal waves which periodically afflict the Pacific coastline. By honouring their dead they were ensuring their benevolence; they were also carrying on age-old traditions and thereby ensuring that they themselves would be honoured and looked after once they died. As for the idea of mummifying the dead, the Chinchorros shared with the ancient Egyptians an arid desert home. Perhaps both peoples observed the effects of the natural desiccation of bodies and eventually stumbled on the notion that they could carry the natural process a stage farther by performing artificial mummification.

reattach the head. Using a paste of white ash, they next remodelled the general shape of the face and body, sometimes wrapping a final layer of reed fibres around the emerging mummy. Then the skin was carefully laid back over the whole assemblage – with the legs they had sometimes simply rolled the skin down like stockings. A wig of short black hair was placed on the head. Finally, a coat of black paint – made from manganese, available locally and ground into a powder using a pestle and mortar – was applied to the entire mummy. All this was probably

BOY MUMMY *This mummy dates from the 'red' epoch in Chinchorro history – from about 2620 BC. By then slightly less trouble was taken in disarticulating and then reassembling the body during mummification. The mummies were daubed with red using a paint extracted from locally available iron oxide.*

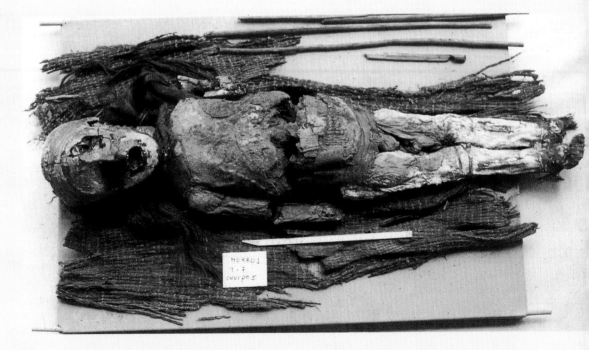

THE FIRST
AUSTRALIANS

The first people in Australia arrived by boat, although experts disagree on where they came from. The early inhabitants dispersed across the whole continent, occupying a range of terrain from coast to highlands, and even the desert interior.

While some parties of humans were pushing northwards into Siberia from north-east Asia around 40 000 years ago, similar bands of early settlers were moving south into Australia. They first came to a region now known as Wallacea, after the British naturalist and explorer Alfred Russel Wallace (1823-1913). This is a complex of islands, straits, seas and other waterways stretching from the Indian Ocean through the Indonesian archipelago to the Philippine Sea. For modern naturalists, it marks a dividing line between the distinctive flora and fauna of Asia and that of Australasia – the Indonesian island of Lombok, for example, which lies to the east of the line, has marsupials (creatures that carry their young in pouches) while Bali, the next island to the west, does not.

For early man, Wallacea had a dual effect. On the one hand, it slowed down his push south and east from the Asian mainland – a push that would eventually take him to Australia. On the other hand, for the bands of humans who did get through Wallacea to Australia, it served to isolate them. While Indonesian islands such as Java were joined to the Asian mainland from time to time, there was always a barrier to Australia. Even when sea levels were at their lowest, watery gaps of at least 40 miles (65 km) and maybe as much as 55-60 miles (90-100 km) between islands separated Australia from the rest of the Old World. Whoever wanted to make it there had somehow to cross the gap.

ON A LOG WITH A DOG

There is a story, known as 'the woman on a log with a dog' hypothesis, echoing Aboriginal myths relating to the origin of the ancestors in the dream time, that proposes that a pregnant woman and her female dog, also pregnant, were in a dugout canoe. They were swept away from a distant shore only to find themselves washed up on a beach somewhere in northern Australia a few days later. The woman was supposed to have given rise to the Australian Aboriginal people and her dog to the native dog, or dingo, which was thought to have arrived on the

ISLAND-HOPPER *Early travellers to Australia may have used mangrove rafts of the type in use in western Australia as recently as the early 20th century.*

continent at the same time as humans. The problem with this story is that there is not a shred of evidence to support it, and indeed it is now known that the dingo did not arrive on the continent until about 4000 years ago. Modern science and new discoveries, however, are beginning to shed more light on the arrival.

One discovery was of 50 000-year-old stone tools at a site at the foot of the Arnhem Land plateau in Australia's Northern Territory. This suggests that people arrived on the continent around 50 000 – and some researchers think as much as 60 000 – years ago. The tools were found on the west side of the plateau by researchers from the University of Wollongong and the Australian National University and they reported the discovery in 1990. Material they uncovered included flakes (fragments that have been chipped off a larger stone while making a tool or weapon), grindstones, quartzite tools and red and yellow ochre. Until these finds, the oldest known traces of human settlement in Australasia had come from Papua New Guinea and were thought to date from 40 000 years ago. The Arnhem Land discovery pushes back the date by maybe 20 000 years.

The island of New Guinea, linked to Australia at various times during the ice ages as sea levels rose and fell, was probably one of many staging posts in this migration. Artefacts found on the Huon Peninsula, on the eastern side of New Guinea, include waisted axes (named for their waist-like profile), flakes and stone cores (stones from which flakes have been chipped off). Some of the waisted axes have grooves, indicating that handles were fitted onto them. Similar examples have been found in Melanesia and mainland Australia. The Huon find, which may be as much as 40 000 years old, includes the oldest-known stone tool to show hafting so far discovered anywhere in the world.

TWO-PRONGED INVASION

It has been suggested that people came to Australia in boats or rafts from two directions – a light-boned people from what is now China through the Philippines and

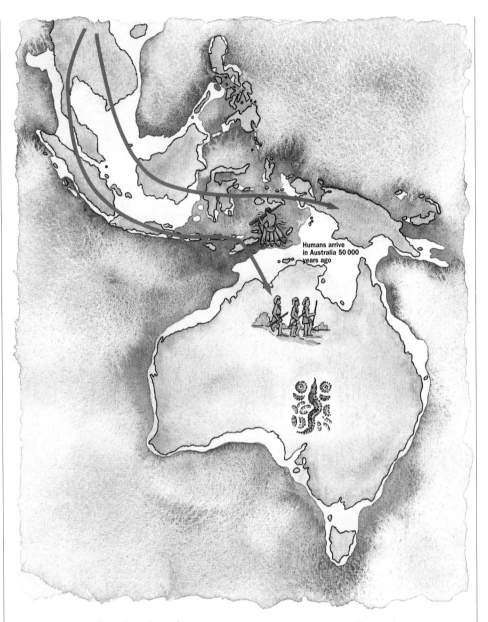

Humans arrive in Australia 50 000 years ago

MIGRATION MAP   Early peoples spread through South-east Asia when sea levels were low and many of today's islands were joined to Asia. Some crossed the sea to Australia.

New Guinea, and a robust-boned group arriving from Java. The evidence was provided by researchers from the Australian National University in Canberra. They were studying the fossil bones of early Aborigines at two locations: Kow Swamp in Victoria, and Lake Mungo in New South Wales. They discovered that certain features, particularly the bones of the skull, were different at the two sites.

The oldest of the Kow Swamp fossils are about 15 000 years old, and they reveal more robust people with thick bones and heavy brow ridges, features that also appear in human remains found in the region around

Java. The Mungo fossils, which are 20 000 years older than the Kow Swamp ones, have a noticeably slighter build. In fact, they suggest people who are less sturdy than modern Aborigines. This more ancient group of migrants may have come from what is now southern China over 40 000 years ago.

One view that is emerging today about

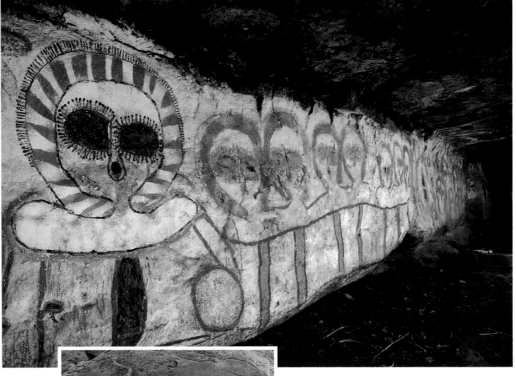

the first Australians is that there were many succeeding groups of migration. These migrations were to an expanded Australia, which at that time included New Guinea. They were composed of bands of people, who must have been capable seafarers, coming through East and South-east Asia. A discovery made at Cossack in western Australia in 1979 lends support to the theory. It consists of the heavy-boned skull of a 40-year-old adult. Similar heavy-boned South-east Asian migrants could have taken a southerly route from Java, through Timor, into the Northern Territory of Australia.

The lighter-boned group might have taken a route through Indochina and Borneo to New Guinea, or reached New Guinea through the Philippines, before arriving at Cape York on the north-east coast of Australia. They would have passed down the east coast, travelling maybe as far as Tasmania, while some groups headed inland.

Subscribers to the theory of successive groups of migrations suggest that as both

STONE AND BONE TOOLS *Tools made from stone and bone have been found at Lake Mungo along with human fossil bones.*

groups were *Homo sapiens*, the populations could have interbred to give rise to the modern Aborigines. Other scientists, however, believe that there was essentially only one founder population in Australia, and that the diversification found in fossils from the sites studied to date developed after man's arrival there.

RAFTING TECHNOLOGY

These biologically modern humans must have used maritime technology to island-hop from Asia to Australia – that is, they must have constructed some kind of watercraft, and they were probably the world's first ocean travellers. Their way of life was based on forests and shorelines, the kind of environment they had come from in Asia. New Guinea and northern Australia had many species of edible plants, molluscs and fish

ANCIENT ART *Rock paintings in Kakadu National Park in the Northern Territory, which include spirit figures (above) and so-called 'X-ray' pictures of a variety of creatures including fish, lizards and insects (right), span 18 000 years. Paints were mixed in special holes in the rocks (left).*

in common that would have been known to these early travellers.

Evidently they occupied a range of terrains. Stone tools, including waisted axes made of volcanic rock, have been found from the coast to the highlands in both New Guinea and northern Australia. Some tools are thought to have been used to ring-bark trees. This would have made the trees die, opening up the canopy and letting in sunlight to stimulate the growth of edible plants, such as yams, sugar cane, bananas and tree fruits. The opening up of the canopy would also have promoted the growth of grass, and this would have fed animals such as kangaroos, which in turn were hunted.

One scholar, Sandra Bowdler, in 1977 proposed that the early settlers kept to the coasts and did not probe the interior of Aus-

GOING FISHING *Early Australians (opposite) used nets to catch fish and shellfish at Lake Mungo. A shell midden at the site (right) represents the accumulated rubbish of human settlement. Overleaf: Lake Mungo and the river that fed it have long since dried up, but the sediments are in the course of erosion, revealing the evidence of early human habitation.*

tralia until 12 000 years ago. However, there is evidence now that human life moved into the challenging desert environment of the interior, by following river valleys inland, at least 22 000 years ago. Stone tools along with some charcoal and red ochre, suggesting an artistic bent, have been found in a rock shelter at Puritjarra in the Cleland Hills. These are low sandstone hills, 47 miles (75 km) west of the main MacDonnell Ranges, in the arid heart of Australia.

That humans came to what is now such a parched area is remarkable. The region was probably one of the most difficult environments that the first Australians encountered. Evidence of human occupation from the Pilbara region of western Australia, the Flinders Ranges and the Strzelecki dunefield indicates that there was widespread human settlement in all these regions by 15 000 to 13 000 years ago.

For food the first desert nomads relied on tubers, such as yams and lily tubers, and other desert plants. The later desert dwellers gathered grass seeds, such as *Panicum composicum* (native millet), which they ground into a flour using sandstone grinding dishes.

AUSTRALIAN ROCK ART

Over the millennia, humans spread out all over Australia. Rock shelters in the Hamersley Plateau in western Australia are believed to be between 26 000 and 21 000 years old. Ochre used at Puritjarra about 22 000

years ago suggests that the distant ancestors of the Australian Aborigines were rock-painting at the same time as the artists of the Lascaux caves, half a world away.

Australian rock art occurs both in rock shelters and on open sandstone platforms

---

AUSTRALIAN BURIALS

Burials took many forms. One, seen at Lake Mungo, southern New South Wales, was to cremate the body, smash the surviving bones and place them in a pit. A second custom was to bury the body in the ground and surround it with stone tools, ochre, shells and animal teeth. A man buried about 7000 years ago in western New South Wales, for example, was adorned with a necklace consisting of 128 pierced teeth of Tasmanian Devils, a species now extinct on the mainland.

---

and vertical panels on cliff faces. In rock shelters the images consist of drawings, paintings, stencils and engravings; in the open, they consist only of rock engravings.

Animals feature strongly at many of the sites. A creature the size of a modern-day rhinoceros, known as Diprotodon, was depicted on a cave wall near Cairns in northern Queensland. It was the world's largest-known marsupial and some experts believe that it lived in Australia and nowhere else until about 6000 years ago, when it became extinct. The painting is thought to be 10 000 years old, indicating that man and Diprotodon lived together for many thousands of years.

In the rest of the world, man's arrival is usually associated with the sudden extinction of large mammals, although in some cases this may be coincidental, but in Australia this has not happened. Experts are not sure why, except that the myths and legends of the modern Aborigines, like those of the Bushmen of southern Africa, show a remarkable degree of respect on the part of these peoples for their fellow creatures. Their forebears evidently learned the secrets of a relatively peaceful coexistence with other animals at an early stage.

OCEAN TRAVELLERS INTO THE PACIFIC

On reaching the eastern shores of South-east Asia, mankind did not stop. With visions of better worlds across the sea, people used rafts or boats to island-hop across the South Pacific, settling where the local resources allowed.

When European navigators set sail to explore the world in the 15th and 16th centuries, they found remarkably few deserted islands. Although a handful, such as Madeira and the Azores in the Atlantic and Mauritius in the Indian Ocean, were still uninhabited by humans, almost every other oceanic island, especially those of Indonesia, the Philippines and across the Pacific, had an existing population of much earlier voyagers. Indeed, the Portuguese explorer Ferdinand Magellan was killed in 1521 during a confrontation with local people in the Philippines. Two and a half centuries later, in 1779, the English navigator Captain James Cook met a similar fate at the hands of Hawaiian islanders.

People used to think that pioneering seafarers, the first inhabitants of the various islands, simply 'drifted' to them quite by

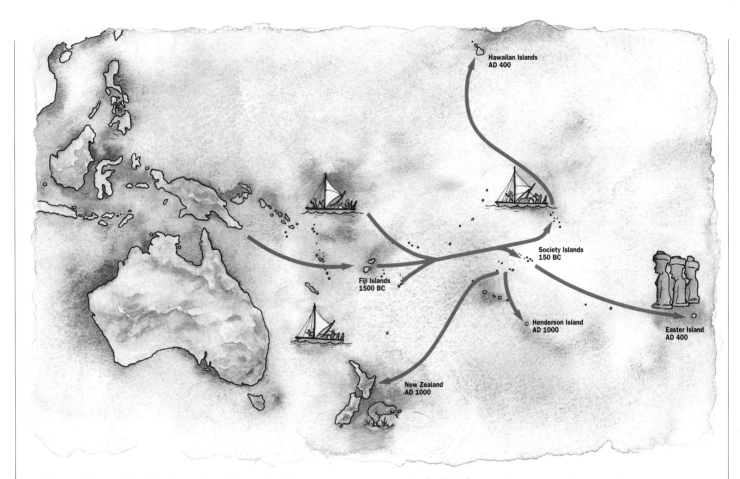

Hawaiian Islands
AD 400

Society Islands
150 BC

Fiji Islands
1500 BC

Henderson Island
AD 1000

Easter Island
AD 400

New Zealand
AD 1000

accident. Most archaeologists today disagree. The invasions were, they believe, the result of deliberate searches for new lands, although achieved with a much less sophisticated technology than the Europeans possessed thousands of years later. Stone-Age people reached the Indonesian islands of Flores and Timor perhaps 100 000 years ago, Australia and New Guinea by 50 000 years ago and the Bismarck Archipelago north-east of New Guinea by 11 000 years ago. From here mankind was ready to take on the Pacific Ocean.

It was people from Indonesia who crossed the Indian Ocean and settled on Madagascar in approximately AD 1000, rather than travellers from the African mainland nearby. Similarly, the early human inhabitants of Hawaii and Easter Is-

ISLAND PARADISE People reached the island of Bora Bora in French Polynesia, in the southern Pacific, about 2000 years ago.

land, two remote outposts in the Pacific, probably arrived by island-hopping from the west, despite the *Kon Tiki* Expedition's brave attempt in 1947 to prove that they could have come from South America.

PIONEER SEAFARERS

Not all voyages were intentional. The short crossing from Indonesia to Australia was probably made by drifting. The prevailing summer winds and currents could easily have swept a raft from Timor or the Moluccas to northern Australia. Survivors clinging on board would have been the first humans to set foot on the Australian continent.

The voyages to the Pacific islands, however, were very different. There is no doubt among archaeologists and seafarers that the journeys were purposeful. Computer simulations and historical records show that it is extremely unlikely that people could have reached eastern Polynesia, say, by accidental drift. Apart from anything else, the predominant wind directions were against them.

Three cave sites on New Ireland in

PEOPLING THE PACIFIC Despite claims that people could have sailed to the Pacific from South America, the probable route was from the west. Overleaf: Polynesians arriving on a Pacific island unload the plants they have brought with them.

northern Melanesia have been found to be 33 000 years old, suggesting that the invasion of Melanesia was going on at roughly the same time that mankind was heading into Australia. The caves contain stone tools, food debris consisting of bones and marine shells, hearths and pits. They also show that humans were able at this early date to cross oceanic straits, for the island was then separated from New Britain (and New Britain from New Guinea) by deep water.

Voyagers from the islands of South-east Asia first 'hopped' their way to the high volcanic islands of western Micronesia, such as *continued on page 98*

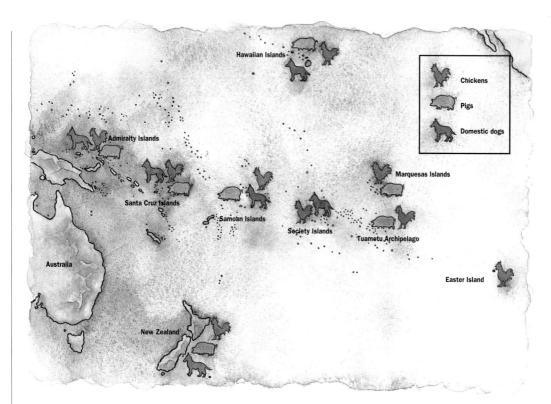

DOMESTICATED ANIMALS *With the travelling people came their animals, whose remains can be found on the islands of the South Pacific.*

Saipan and Guam in the Marianas, by about 4000 years ago. Thereafter, complex societies developed all across Micronesia among its 3000 mainly coral atoll islands scattered over 2.9 million sq miles (7.4 million km²) of ocean. Pottery remains – the oldest being finely made pots in the style known to archaeologists as 'Marianas Red' – are further evidence suggesting a link with the islands of South-east Asia, such as the Philippines, where similar pottery has been found. Some 1500-year-old animal remains include the oldest evidence of the domesticated pig in Micronesia, and limestone pillars, introduced about 1100 years ago, indicate a shift from wood to stone in house construction.

Studies of the languages of Micronesia suggest that a second wave of settlers came from the south, from Melanesia, to inhabit the atolls of Kiribati and the raised reefs of Nauru and Banaba (Ocean Island). The same linguistic studies suggest that the ancestors of today's Polynesians moved westwards from Micronesia. Archaeologists studying pottery remains, however, have come to different conclusions, strongly favouring the Melanesian route to Polynesia.

The seafarers who struck out towards Polynesia are known to scholars as the Lapi-

ta people – after a site in New Caledonia where some of their pottery was found. If the archaeologists' view is the correct one, these people probably left Melanesia about 4000 years ago in single or double outrigger canoes. Such were their navigational skills that they were able to make round trips between parent and daughter colonies. Hunting, fishing and crop growing enabled the new colonies to survive. Within 2000 years they had colonised the rest of Oceania, a feat now recognised as one of the most far-reaching and rapid prehistoric migrations.

CROSSING THE OCEAN VASTNESS

The Polynesian islands must have been discovered during a series of upwind voyages that reached Fiji, Samoa and Tonga by around 3000 years ago, the Marquesas by 2150 years ago, and all the other Polynesian islands during the next 500

ANCIENT NAVIGATION *The early Polynesian seafarers constructed maps showing the positions of islands, ocean currents and swells.*

years. Previous excursions had involved water gaps, between the major groups of islands west of Vanuatu and New Caledonia, that were no more than about 300 miles (480 km) wide. Settlers had been able to return to their mother colonies for materials and help.

But these later voyages were greater than any before undertaken anywhere in the world, across many miles of open ocean: 750 miles (1200 km) from Samoa to the nearest of the Cook Islands; 620 miles (1000 km) from there to the Society Islands; another 870 miles (1400 km) to the Marquesas Islands, and a further 2175 miles (3500 km) to Hawaii. The voyagers could not return home easily if the going got tough.

There are no native mammals, apart from bats, east of the Solomon Islands. Native snakes are absent east of Samoa, and large-bodied lizards do not occur east of Fiji. Archaeological evidence suggests that local bird populations, sea turtles, fish and shellfish sustained the early settlers. Fishhooks of a type not seen elsewhere have been found at archaeological sites on the Marquesas, together with the bones of bot-

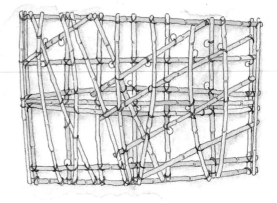

tom-dwelling inshore fish. These suggest that the early Polynesians were experimenting with new fishing techniques. Whale and porpoise bones recovered from sites at Fa'ahia on Huahine Island in the Tahiti archipelago indicate that fish were not the only large animals taken from the sea.

The Polynesians did not, however, have everything their own way. With their seafaring and navigational skills, they could have conquered the entire Pacific, but they failed to do so. Although they populated all the uninhabited islands from Tonga eastwards, including New Zealand, they could not force their way onto islands with resident populations. In the New Hebrides and Caroline Islands they were able to gain a toehold only on uninhabited, outlying islands as the others were already inhabited by the Melanesians and Micronesians.

IMPACT IN THE PACIFIC

The invasion of the south-western Pacific by the Polynesians had a profound impact on the islands. They introduced crops and domestic animals throughout Polynesia, proof that their patterns of settlement were as thoroughly planned as the actual voyages of exploration. These early voyagers left their home ports with the intention not just of wandering the Pacific but of settling down and living elsewhere.

On the other hand, their use of indigenous animals for food, combined with the predations of rats introduced from southern Asia, had devastating effects on the animal populations of the islands, particularly sea birds that nested on the ground and land birds that thrived in virgin forests.

Birds, turtles and large-bodied lizards took the brunt of the exploitation. Many became extinct. When the Polynesians arrived in Hawaii about 1500 years ago, they exterminated seven species of geese, one species of sea eagle, seven flightless rails, two large crows and three species of owls. Before their

TRAVELLING PIGS
The Polynesians did not rely on the native fauna for food, but took pigs, which they fed on coconuts.

invasion Hawaii had twice as many species of birds.

Prehistoric man, often thought of as a natural conservationist, was often in reality a destroyer of natural resources. On Ua Huka in the Marquesas, 8 out of 20 species

---

THOSE IN PERIL ON THE SEA

Detailed modern studies of Polynesian navigation techniques, together with a Hawaii-to-Tahiti sea trial of a reconstructed Polynesian canoe named *Hokule'a*, have demonstrated that exploring the Pacific was well within the voyaging capabilities of the Polynesians. But despite the evident confidence of these early seafarers and the skills with which they navigated the islands of the Pacific, there must have been heavy losses. Some experts have estimated that the settlement of Polynesia cost 500 000 Polynesian lives at sea.

---

of sea birds, including petrels, boobies and shearwaters, together with 14 out of 16 species of land birds, including flightless rails, pigeons, doves, parrots and songbirds, were wiped out. On New Zealand, which was colonised by the Polynesians about 1000 years ago, 30 bird species, including 13

species of moa and nine other flightless birds, vanished before the Europeans arrived.

Further evidence of destruction comes from all over the Pacific, including the remotest outposts. Henderson Island is an example – a very small and remote dot of land with an area of just 14 sq miles (37 km²), lying near Pitcairn Island in the centre of the South Pacific. This area of ocean and its island used to be thought of as a part of the world little affected by human activity – but the Polynesians were there, albeit briefly. They arrived about 1000 years ago from Mangareva Island, 250 miles (400 km) to the west, attracted by untapped resources of fish and shellfish, nesting sea birds, flightless birds, pigeons and sea turtles. They imported coconut trees, swamp taro (a plant with a large edible root), candlenut trees, banana plants and sweet potatoes. No more than 50 people may have settled on the island but they had a devastating effect on the wildlife. The evidence comes from debris found in caves and rock shelters on the north shore. Scientists from the USA who visited the island in 1985 discovered the remains of birds and animals that no longer exist there.

The main food for the settlers must have been pigeons, the small Society Island's pigeon and the large 28 oz (800 g) Marquesas

pigeon. Both have been eaten to extinction on Henderson, but are living elsewhere in the Pacific.

The bird populations of Henderson Island were probably devastated because there was little else to eat. The traditional Polynesian foods of taro, breadfruit, sweet potato and pork could not be harvested here successfully because the terrain was unsuitable. When the numbers of birds declined, the settlers left.

The evidence from artefacts found on the islands shows that, until then, the people of Henderson relied on trade with Mangareva and Pitcairn to make up for the resources they lacked, but events on the mother island put paid to this. Mangareva's

LOCAL AGRICULTURE
Polynesians plant yams, a staple part of their diet from earliest times, on cleared land.

landscape had itself been so badly devastated by its human inhabitants that food resources were scarce and the surviving people ended their time in an orgy of war. The trade with Henderson ended and the Henderson islanders, forced to rely on their own resources, found them sadly lacking. They survived for six generations, but by AD 1600 the last humans there had died out.

Elsewhere in the Pacific, devastation of an island's natural resources was followed by a change in which the inhabitants started keeping domestic pigs and dogs and growing crops, such as breadfruit. Forests were destroyed for agriculture, and flightless ground-nesting birds were hunted to extinction by animals the Polynesians had introduced to the islands.

This change brought another transformation, in the way societies were organised. With settlements established and natural resources depleted by over-exploitation, com-

munities came to be dominated by the chiefs, who used taboos to control access to the remaining food resources. Pork and dog meat were reserved for high-ranking men; women were allowed to eat dog only on certain ceremonial occasions.

On Hawaii, fish stocks were kept up by the use of large fish ponds. About 450 were dug, and they were estimated to provide more than 2 million lb (910 000 kg) of fish each year. In fact, this was one of the few conservation success stories associated with human settlement in the Pacific. While the land fauna of islands was being mismanaged, fish stocks were being controlled by rigorous conservation measures. Polynesians and Micronesians had closed seasons, restricted areas and size restrictions centuries before such measures were introduced in Europe and North America.

THE DAWN OF CIVILISATION

3

ANCIENT HIGH-RISE *Jericho was one of the world's earliest cities.*

ONE OF THE FEATURES THAT SETS MANKIND APART FROM THE REST OF THE NATURAL WORLD IS THE WAY IN WHICH HE HAS DEVELOPED ACTIVITIES SUCH AS ART, MUSIC, WRITING, RELIGION AND SCIENCE — SKILLS AND IDEAS THAT ARE UNNECESSARY FOR SURVIVAL, BUT WHICH ARE THE TRAPPINGS OF WHAT WE REFER TO AS 'CIVILISATION'. AS WELL AS FINDING ALL MANNER OF SUBJECTS FOR OUR ADVANCED BRAINS TO THINK ABOUT, WE HAVE ALSO FOUND WAYS OF MAKING LIFE EASIER FOR OURSELVES: ALTHOUGH MANY ANIMALS, INCLUDING MAMMALS,

EARLY IMAGES *The Makwa cave paintings from Zimbabwe.*

BIRDS AND INSECTS, USE TOOLS, ONLY MANKIND HAS TAKEN THINGS A STEP FARTHER WITH THE DEVELOPMENT OF TECHNOLOGY AND ENGINEERING.

ART AND EXPRESSION

The painting and sculpting of everyday objects, such as wild animals and human figures, by Stone Age people came as a shock to historians, who thought that quality works of art first appeared much later, with the ancient Egyptians.

In 1940, four teenage boys searching for a lost dog found their way into a series of caves in the Dordogne region of south-west France. They discovered hundreds of paintings of animals on the walls and ceiling – the work of primitive rock artists about 17000 years ago. Fat horses with frizzy manes galloped past the enormous figure of a white bull, an auroch, a species of wild cattle (probably the ancestor of today's domesticated cattle) that is now extinct. Running in the opposite direction were three small stags with finely painted antlers; the shape and texture of the rock on which they were painted gave the impression that they were running through water. This was Lascaux's Hall of the Bulls, now one of the most famous examples of Stone Age art.

It was created by Cro-Magnon artists, who decorated the walls of many caves in

the Dordogne, the French Pyrenees and Cantabria on the northern coast of Spain between 30 000 and 10 000 years ago – a period when Europe was caught in the grip of an Ice Age. In addition to their work at Lascaux, Cro-Magnon artists left beautiful images at Niaux in the Pyrenees, Cougnac in France and Altamira in Spain. Some of the paintings were of magical beasts – Les Trois Frères cave in the Pyrenees, for example, has a creature known as 'the sorcerer' with a man's head, the antlers of a stag and the tail of a horse – but most were of real animals that were living at that time in southern Europe.

There were also paintings of people. In Lascaux's Hall of Bulls there is only one person, a male character with the head or mask of a bird, but elsewhere human figures are more common. They tend to be like the images of L.S. Lowry, stick-like figures or stylised line drawings. About 78 per cent of them, possibly males, are running or hunting, carrying or throwing spears or on the receiving end of them. Some figures, which possibly represent females, are passive, and are usually in groups. The paintings appear

EXTINCT *A painting at Lascaux records the auroch, a species of wild cattle that became extinct in 1627. A necklace of shells and the teeth of wild cattle and small carnivores (below) probably adorned an ancient neck.*

HUNTER AND HUNTED *In an ancient rock painting an elephant or mastodon is confronted by a human hunter, the event recorded for all time.*

to suggest a society in which men went hunting while women stayed in all-female groups, raising children, gathering food and socialising, but this is not conclusively so.

MYSTERIOUS PAINTINGS

What did this wonderful art mean and what does it tell us about the people who created it? At the beginning of the 20th century the priest and archaeologist the Abbé Henri Breuil suggested that it was a form of hunting magic, a way of capturing the animals by sorcery in the hope that it would make the beasts more vulnerable to hunters. Another possibility was proposed by the anthropologist André Leroi-Gourhan. According to him, the pictures were symbolic depictions of the way in which the Palaeolithic people viewed the world – a world divided between male and female.

Femaleness, Leroi-Gourhan suggested, was represented by animals such as the bison and aurochs, which were often juxtaposed with human figures in the paintings. Maleness was embodied by the horse and the ibex. This somewhat Freudian approach was linked to sexual symbolism in the pictures, such as geometric designs placed one inside the other. An arrow-shaped symbol entering a V-shaped wound was interpreted as a male symbol entering a female one.

The problem with these two approaches is that a single notion is unlikely to explain what motivated artists across 25 000

years of activity. It is more probable that artists were inspired and influenced by many things.

More recently, scientists have examined the animal paintings and compared the number of times they appear on the walls with the number of associated artefacts and bones in the caves. This has led to new hypotheses. In one site in the Dordogne, a team of American researchers from the University of West Virginia examined 90 caves, containing 1955 animal portraits and 151 sites with signs of human settlement. They counted all the bones they found of reindeer, horses, ibex, mammoths, bison, aurochs and a host of smaller mammals. They discovered that the numbers of bones from smaller mammals were in proportion to the number of times they appeared on the cave walls. The larger mammals, however, were de-

continued on page 106

WRITING AND RECORDS

The earliest-known writing in the world dates from about 3300 BC and comes from the site of the ancient city of Uruk, in what is now southern Iraq. It helped the local administration to cope with the city's increasing wealth and complexity, stirred apparently by the timeless instinct to collect tax. The writing is on baked clay tablets and consists of pictographs, symbols representing, for example, a head of barley along with dots representing numerals. These tablets probably recorded tax payments of crops received from farmers. Later, the pictograph system was transformed into the first wedge-shaped cuneiform script – a system so successful that it was eventually used in Babylon and Persia. Indeed, writing as we now use it in the West has its roots in this script.

Uruk was one of many city-states that arose, about 5000 years ago, in Mesopotamia, the area of south-western Asia between the Euphrates and Tigris rivers. Together these city-states formed the inventive Sumerian civilisation. The cities had systematic division of labour (with specialist workers assigned to different tasks), built impressive monuments, had an organised religion and depended on satellite agricultural settlements to provide them with food. Writing was developed to underpin their bureaucracy, record their transactions, keep track

WRITTEN RECORDS This cuneiform tablet (above right), from 2050 BC, is a receipt for copper and bronze tools. Reeds, abundant in the marshlands of Mesopotamia, provided styluses. Scribes started at the top left of a tablet and worked down in columns. An oracle bone from about 2000 BC (below right) shows Chinese writing in its earliest form. People wrote questions about the future on the bone and then heated it until it cracked. From the shape of the crack, a diviner deduced the answer to the question.

of goods and for stocktaking.

By around 2500 BC, the Mesopotamians were using the first cuneiform script. Scribes found it easier to draw straight lines in clay than the irregular shapes of objects as in the earlier pictographs, and so they started to use wedge-shaped (cuneiform) styluses of reed to make wedge-shaped lines. At first, the shorthand was still recognisable as a form of pictographs, but gradually the figures became more abstract, each sign representing a word. As the use of writing spread beyond record-keeping, however, it was found that some concepts were more difficult than others to represent in signs or symbols. Thus, a few signs came to stand for more than one thing: the foot sign meant 'to stand' in one context, 'to go' in another.

Such was the importance of writing that schools for scribes were set up, where scholars learnt 2000 or more different signs. The tasks they undertook expanded. Some composed epics and hymns; others wrote about their own experiences. And some became mathematicians.

Ancient Mesopotamian maths is with us to this day. It was based on 60 – rather as

CARVED IN STONE Pictograms, from around 3000 BC, record offerings at a temple. Unlike most other early pictograms, they are engraved in stone rather than clay. Stone, more durable than clay, was widely used in later times to record, for example, the achievements of great kings.

our system is based on 100 – a number which has the advantage of being divisible by many others. We still have 60 seconds in a minute and 60 minutes in an hour. A multiple of 60 divides the circle and the compass into degrees, and a factor of it, 12, splits the year into months.

Later, similar cuneiform systems were developed all over the Middle East, and their interpretation has increased our knowledge of many aspects of life at that time. On a Sumerian clay tablet, dating from 2250 BC, for example, a medical text describes the treatment for an unknown ailment. It suggests that 'strong beer is poured over resin and heated over a fire; this is mixed with river bitumen oil and the concoction given to the sick person to drink'.

The Mesopotamians were not the only people to devise systems of writing. The Egyptians had hieroglyphs, using figures or pictures to represent words or sounds. This script was almost as old as the Mesopotamian one, dating to around 3100 BC. Farther east, the earliest evidence for the use of Chinese pictographs dates from about 1200 BC. In the Americas, the Maya civilisation of modern Mexico and Guatemala had a kind of alphabet in which hieroglyph-like symbols stood not for letters, but for syllables. The first evidence for this script dates back to 600 BC. Farther south, the people of the Andes had no alphabet, but they did use *quipus*, systems of knotted strings with which officials of the Inca Empire kept track of an astonishing network of storehouses spread across their mountain realms. Specialised *quipucamayocs* kept detailed records of all the crops, textiles and other goods contained in even the most far-flung provincial storehouses. Wherever complex societies arose, the need to keep records arose with them, each culture devising its own special system.

SOLVING THE RIDDLE
The Rosetta Stone (left) commemorates the first anniversary of the reign of the Egyptian Pharaoh Ptolemy V in 196 BC. It is inscribed in three scripts: two versions of Egyptian hieroglyphics and the Greek alphabet. Starting from the Greek script, 19th-century scholars, notably the Frenchman Jean-François Champollion, were able to decipher the hieroglyphics.

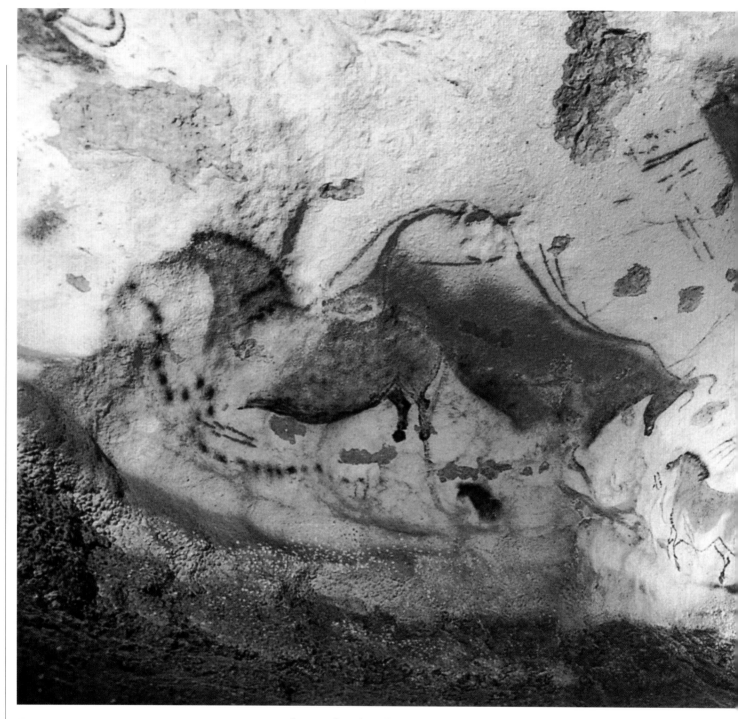

ROOF OF LIFE *Using 12*
pigments, the artists of the
Lascaux caves painted more
than 600 pictures of horses,
deer, cattle and other animals.

picted more often than the numbers of
their bones would have suggested. There
seemed to be a correlation between the
numbers of paintings and of bones, but the
size of the animals also seemed to be taken
into account, the heavier animals being rep-

resented more often than the smaller ones.
It stimulated the researchers to suggest a variety of theories about the paintings.

One theory has it that the pictures are a
kind of calendar of natural events occurring
in the world around them. Another suggests
that they represent a guide to animals useful as food – hence the interest in size.
There is another plausible explanation. Pictures of the ibex, a mountain goat living in
Europe and the Middle East, appeared
more frequently than could be accounted

for by its bone count. The researchers hit on
an interesting idea: could the pictures also
relate to animals that are aggressive to man?

They asked wildlife specialists to rate the
animals painted on the cave walls according
to their aggressiveness. The ibex, though a
small animal, was rated as dangerous. Deer
were rated less menacing and, significantly, appeared on the walls less frequently
than their bone count would suggest. The
paintings, so the interpretation goes, were
there to impress upon the minds of young

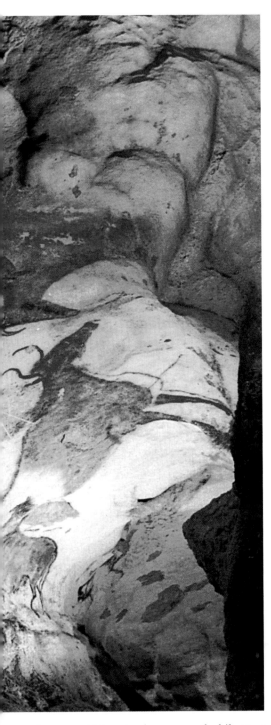

characteristic position – no mean feat of observation.

KNOW YOUR NATURAL HISTORY

These ancient peoples clearly had an intimate understanding of the natural history of the animals they hunted. This is confirmed at another notable Stone Age site at La Solutré in France. On the evidence of many thousands of horse skeletons found there, it was a place where ancient man slaughtered horses in the deep, narrow valleys that run down from the high plateau of the Massif Central towards the Saône river.

At first, scientists believed that early man had herded the horses and driven them over the steep cliffs that drop away from the ridges between the valleys. According to the original interpretation, the horses plunged to their deaths and were butchered by the human hunters for food. But researchers from the Virginia Museum of Natural History think otherwise.

For one thing, horses tend to live in small groups rather than large herds, and it is unlikely that humans on foot could gather together several groups and drive them over a cliff. Another point is that the remains are not found at the foot of the steep cliffs but on the other side of the valley. This would have meant hauling every corpse across the valley to butcher it, an improbable scenario.

The more likely explanation is that the horses went on seasonal migrations. They spent the winter on the open plain but avoided the biting flies and high temperatures of summer by heading for the mountains. The trek took them through the valleys and the human hunters were waiting for them. The horses were diverted from their normal route by man-made barriers of branches and rocks, and trapped in a cul-de-sac where they were killed with spears and butchered.

Showing as they do elements of animal behaviour such as migration, mating and feeding habits, as well as the ferocity of different species and their usefulness as food, the cave paintings record information that humans living in the area needed to know in order to survive. Clearly, they contained information that needed to be passed on from one generation to the next.

RESOUNDING CAVES

French researchers studying 20 000-year-old cave sites in the department of Ariège in the French Pyrenees discovered that the prehistoric artists painted more pictures in caves in which sounds, including musical notes, resonate, or are intensified and prolonged through vibration, than in those where they do not, and have suggested that music may have played a part in ancient ritual.

They made their find while whistling and singing in various octaves while walking through cave systems. They then decided to produce a map; when they found a resonant spot, they marked it on a map and sang on. They then compared the acoustic map with a map of the cave paintings and found that they matched. Indeed, they revealed that most paintings are found within 1 yd (1 m) of a point of resonance in each cave. In one cave, the Grotte de Portel, the resonant point of the chamber is marked by a series of red dots since there is no

---

LASCAUX PIGMENTS

The colours in the rock paintings at Lascaux were created using materials found within a radius of 9 miles (15 km) from the caves. Local minerals were ground and mixed to create a wide range of hues. Haematite or iron oxide was mined for shades of red, and manganese oxide for black. The crystal structure of the compounds was important. Sticks of black manganese could be used for long, dark lines to outline large objects such as bulls, but the red colour was put on in a thick slurry of water, clay and haematite covering smaller areas, such as small depictions of horses.

---

room for a full-sized painting. The fact that the position of the dots coincides with that of maximum resonance is unlikely to be coincidence.

The image of ancient peoples shuffling

---

hunters which animals were worthwhile to kill and which ones caused the most trouble.

Whatever the reason, the artists had observed the animals closely. Postures, the physical details of body, limbs, horns, antlers and the like are meticulously drawn. Even seasonal changes in the fur are noted, as are particular aspects of animal behaviour. In the Lascaux caves, bison are depicted moulting their winter coat, while stags swimming across a river are portrayed with their heads held up and tilted back in the and chanting and painting images that represent their knowledge of the natural world is an intriguing one. They might even have played simple instruments. Flutes from animal toe-bones and what could be percussion instruments have been found in several cave sites. The painters themselves may have formed an elite group dedicated to their art and possessing special knowledge. They were not alone, however, in their skill at representing the world around them.

ART IN AFRICA

Rock paintings in the isolated Tassili-N'Ajjer mountains of the Sahara Desert represent four successive cultures. These ancient works of art show camels, horses with chariots, cattle, and curious round-headed figures with featureless faces and flared leggings. There are 4000 or more of them in all, the oldest of which date from 12 000 years ago.

In East Africa, rock art estimated to be about 10 000 years old, some of the oldest in East Africa, was painted on granite boulders, found by the palaeontologist Mary Leakey at Kondoa in central Tanzania in

DESERT GALLERY   *In the Tassili mountains in the Sahara, rock paintings of people and animals reveal that this area was not always a desert. Among those depicted is a horned animal (below), probably a Barbary sheep, a species that lives in North Africa to this day.*

1935. The pictures show animals such as ostriches, giraffes, antelope (particularly eland), elephants, rhinos and large snakes resembling Egyptian cobras, together with people dancing, playing instruments and hunting. The sites for this art tend to be gigantic boulders, although some paintings are found on the walls of rock shelters, shallow caves and cliff overhangs. The pigments used were mainly ochre, manganese and bird droppings mixed together with animal fat, which enabled them to last for a very long time. Indeed, ochre 'pencils', consisting of ground pigment mixed with grease, were discovered in deposits near one of the sites.

The people, like those in other Stone Age paintings, seem to be segregated. Groups that appear to be dancing and playing instruments are composed mainly of women. Men feature as hunters. The animals represented are similar to those found in modern East Africa, and tend to include ones that are potential food. The lion is included, not as food but probably as an animal to fear.

Southern Africa has also revealed an extraordinary concentration of rock paintings, in Namibia's highest range, the Brandberg Mountains. The climatic conditions here are less extreme than in the nearby eastern part of the Central Namib Desert, and so it was favourable to prehis-

toric settlers, offering a diversity of habitats for edible animals and plants.

The sites, which have been excavated by German researchers from the University of Cologne, have the remains of stone tools, pottery, bones, ostrich eggshells, plant remains and charcoal. The paintings themselves are difficult to date, but it is thought that many are between 3500 and 2000 years old. In one 1076 sq ft (100 m²) rock shelter, known as the 'Giant Cave', there are more than 1000 individual paintings. These include a large, red-painted human figure on the ceiling with fragments of paint peeling off. These were dated using the radiocarbon method and the painting proved to be 2700 years old.

In southern Namibia, in the rock shelter known as Apollo 11, painted slabs were found that are 28 000 to 25 000 years old, the oldest-known rock art in Africa.

THE FIRST SCULPTORS

The western European cave sites that contain art are dominated by rock paintings, the province of Cro-Magnon artists, the so-called Franco-Cantabrian 'school'. Eastern Europe, meanwhile, has sites containing portable art, such as clay figurines and carvings in bone and ivory, most of them simple but realistic representations of wild animals. The Vogelherd horse, for exam-

ple, carved from mammoth ivory, is about 29 000 years old and is one of the oldest-known animal carvings found at Vogelherd in Germany. But, there are also some human figures, mainly female, carved or moulded from locally available materials. Female statuettes most often portray a 'Venus' figure – so named after the Roman goddess of love. They are highly stylised and accentuate the parts of the body related to sexuality and fertility. The breasts are large, as are the hips.

Archaeologists have attempted to explain these statuettes – both animal and human – and the favoured conclusion is that they were a way of gaining some control, albeit symbolic, over the vastness of nature. In effect, they reduced nature to a portable size. The process of making the statuette brought with it power over either the animal it represented or the force, such as fertility, it symbolised.

THE FIRST JEWELLERY

On a smaller scale, and still more portable, is jewellery. A concern with bodily adornment, a characteristic of all known human societies, is evident from the archaeological record from around 35 000 years ago, and was widespread across Europe and in other regions as far away as Australia. The Aurignacian period, which lasted from 44 000 to

NAMIBIAN GALLERY *Rock engravings by the San (Bushman) people can be seen in Twyfelfontein, Damaraland. They depict animals of the region (below), including wildebeest, giraffe and rhinoceros.*

SCULPTURES *A horse and bison are cut into rock at Le Roc de Sers, Charente, France. The mammoth (above) at Vogelherd is carved from mammoth ivory.*

OBESE WOMAN *The female 'Venus' figurine has exaggerated features that experts thought were associated with fertility.*

18 000 years ago, shows the greatest abundance of prehistoric jewellery.

Sites from this period reveal adornments, mostly beads and pendants made of soft stone, ivory, shell and tooth, alongside sophisticated stone, bone and antler tools. These included high-quality flint bladelets used for scraping, bone and antler awls (pointed tools for piercing wood and leather), wedges and spear points. In the early Aurignacian period, the adornments are found in a working environment, such as in camp sites; later they are associated with burials. Later again, at Sungir near Moscow, long lines of ivory beads and pierced teeth have been found on the remains of several ancient people and dated to a time between 28 000 and 24 000 years ago. At the 30 000-year-old site at Cro-Magnon in south-western France, bodies have been found with pierced shells and an ivory pendant.

Materials for body adornments are rarely found close by. More usually, the sources are many miles away. Whether the materials were obtained by travel or trade will probably remain unknown, but great value must have been placed on them, and they were displayed with honour. Most probably the adornments had some type of social significance, establishing rank, position or authority.

Teeth came mainly from predatory animals, such as the wolf and bear, although there is a site in former Czechoslovakia that had necklaces exclusively of beaver teeth. It is assumed that people wearing such adornments hoped to evoke the spirit and power of these creatures.

Prehistoric images are not exclusively representations of figures and animals: the oldest-known abstract image dates from well before this period. It appears on a 300 000-year-old ox rib from France, on which a series of connected, festooned double arcs have been carved. Of about the same age is a coastal shelter in southern France, which would have been occupied in springtime, where traces of red ochre have been found. This may have been used for ritualistic body decoration, one of the most vivid yet least durable forms of artistic expression. Both finds must have been the work of descendants of *Homo erectus*.

Curiously, although *Homo sapiens* probably evolved in Africa more than 100 000 years ago, it is not until 40 000 years ago that anything created by them appears that is definitely symbolic. The apparently sudden arrival of 'art' – beads, pendants, ornaments, rock paintings – provided the world's first representational images. They appeared during one of the greatest periods of technological and social innovation in all history, suggesting that inventiveness and the ability to represent images went hand in hand. In addition, by 30 000 years ago, the amount of information one generation wanted to pass on to the next would have become considerable. Art must have been the answer to a social need. It ensured that rules could not be forgotten, possibly acting as a kind of tribal encyclopedia or even an ancient 'survival course'.

AUSTRALIA'S ABORIGINAL ART

The rock art galleries of Australia are more than simple expressions of aesthetic creativity. They are vivid, yet tangible, records of the continent's natural history. They even depict animals that are now extinct, such as a species of echidna – a burrowing, egg-laying mammal with a spiny coat – thought to have disappeared 25 000 to 15 000 years ago. A drawing on the ceiling of a cave in northern Queensland is believed to show a Diprotodon, a rhinoceros-sized marsupial which became extinct between 35 000 and 6000 years ago. At Ubirr, 22 miles (35 km) north-east of Jabiru, a rock drawing of the recently extinct thylacine or Tasmanian tiger was discovered.

Ubirr is in the Kakadu National Park, near Darwin in the Northern Territory. It is one of the largest such parks in Australia and it also contains the most extensive collection of Aboriginal art. Here, local fishes, such as the barramundi, as well as saltwater crocodiles and sea turtles are drawn as if they had been X-rayed, the internal bones seemingly represented by crisscross lines. In the colourful, crowded montages, animals carry baskets or spears as if they were humans, while real humans are also depicted hunting and dancing.

Rock art appears all over Australia. From the deserts of the centre to the continent's northern tip, the mythology and stories of

the local people are depicted in paintings in caves or rock overhangs. They show, for example, the legendary red-backed parrot woman who announced that the Dreamtime of Creation, the golden age when the Earth received its present form, was coming to an end. In the traditional Aboriginal view of the world, every feature of the land and every creature living in or on it has a role to play. Gorges, troughs and depressions, all represent the traces left by great supernatural beings.

ROCK LINES *Geometrical patterns have been daubed on rocks in the Macdonnell Ranges of central Australia. They mark sacred sites.*

This painting tradition of the first Australians is generally thought to have its origins about 20 000 years ago. Geometric drawings and animal tracks on the rocks of dark underground passages at Koonalda have been dated to this period. But there is also circumstantial evidence that the first painters were producing their art at an even earlier date. Red ochre, of the kind used by the painters, has been found in the oldest sediments of a painted rock shelter in northern Australia, estimated to be 50 000 years old. This is not definite proof, how-ever, that artists were at work because the local people of the Gulf country of northern Australia also used red ochre when packing wild plums, in order to preserve them.

Whatever the age the earliest antipodean art proves to be, it was being produced at roughly the same time that the first European artists were adorning the walls and ceilings of France's Lascaux caves and Spain's Altamira caves. Mankind's cultural development was evidently progressing along a broad geographical front. There is,

HAND PAINTING *Hand prints form part of an unusual mural in Queensland's Carnarvon Gorge National Park. A modern Aboriginal artist uses similar effects in a mural in Kakadu National Park.*

SEE-THROUGH ART *Fish and turtles, painted in the 'X-ray style', feature in rock art from Kakadu's Nourlangie Rock. The original artists, living some 6000 years ago, took refuge in a shelter in Nourlangie Rock during the wet season.*

however, a significant difference between north and south. The European tradition died out at the end of the last Ice Age about 10 000 years ago, but true Aboriginal rock artists have died within living memory, and the tradition continues today through bark painting. Moreover, many rock paintings have been repainted several times over the centuries, renewing their original colours and outlines. Interestingly, when the first rock paintings were found in the Dordogne and Cantabria more than 100 years ago, the scholars of the day turned to Australian Aboriginals for guidance in deciphering their discoveries.

SELF-SUFFICIENCY: THE FIRST FARMERS

Agriculture has a longer history than was first thought.

As part of the process of harnessing nature, ancient people domesticated animals and grew crops, while gathering in ever larger communities that sometimes came into conflict.

Some of the biggest questions in the story of mankind relate to a period between 10 000 and 5000 years ago. With the last Ice Age coming to an end, and the glaciers receding, the climate was growing warmer and wetter. At some time during this period, a few groups of people started to abandon their ancient way of life, based on hunting game and gathering nuts and fruits, and settle down as farmers.

Farming's birthplace has traditionally been ascribed to the 'fertile crescent' of Mesopotamia, an area stretching from the Persian Gulf along the banks of the Tigris and Euphrates rivers as far as the Mediterranean coast. Here, the traditional theory goes, the locals learned to sow and harvest cereal crops such as wheat and barley about 10 000 years ago. They produced an abundance of food, which enabled them to live in permanent communities that later grew into the complex civilisations of the Mediterranean and Middle East. Now, however, evidence that people were gradually learning to cultivate crops much earlier than 10 000 years ago suggests that things were never quite so simple.

In the Middle East alone cereals and pulses were used intensively by around 12 000 years ago, and by about 10 000 years ago domestic varieties of peas, lentils, barley and emmer (a kind of wheat) had appeared. The change from the wild to the domesticated strains of these plants was often rapid

HORTICULTURAL BEGINNINGS
A model of a farmer ploughing with two oxen was discovered in an Egyptian tomb dated about 2000 BC.

but never uniform – some localities continued to use wild strains long after domestic forms were common in neighbouring areas. None the less, by 8000 years ago, many people in the Middle East were cultivating domestic wheat and barley, although many others continued the hunter-gatherer way of life.

Elsewhere, sorghum and millet are thought to have become important food crops in Africa by about 8000 years ago. Seeds that closely resemble domesticated sorghum and millet, rather than the wild varieties, have been found at sites in southern Egypt, providing the earliest evidence of the use of these cereal plants.

WINE AND BEER: PIONEER DRINKERS

The first known wine and beer drinkers in the world were the ancient Sumerians who lived in Lower Mesopotamia around 6000 years ago. They developed irrigation in order to grow domesticated cereals, including barley, from which they made a kind of beer. At Godin Tepe, a site in the Zagros Mountains of north-western Iran, a jug was found with crisscross grooves inside it, probably designed to retain beer sediments. A pale yellow residue was scraped from some of the grooves and it proved to be chemically similar to the principal component of 'beerstone', a substance that settles out on the surfaces of fermentation tanks used to make barley beer. The earliest signs of the production of grape wine were found at the same site.

From an even earlier period, grinding stones have been found at a site at Wadi Kubbaniya, Egypt, which may be as much as 18 000-17 000 years old. These could have been used for grinding wild grain, but there is certainly evidence that at later periods African people were raising wheat, barley, lentils, chickpeas, capers and dates at Wadi Kubbaniya. On the other side of the world, between 10 000 and 7000 years ago, predominantly hunter-gatherer communities were tending plants in the highlands of

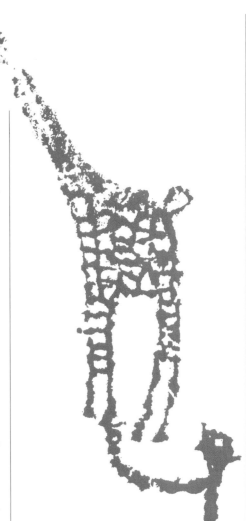

TIED GIRAFFE *A rock engraving at Jebel Uweinat shows a giraffe tethered to a post. Overleaf: Villagers are building a new farmstead in an early farming settlement in the modern Netherlands – around 5000 BC.*

modern Papua New Guinea where drainage ditches and crude fields have been found.

In the Americas, a primitive form of maize (corn) was cultivated in Mexico more than 7000 years ago, and in 1989 evidence emerged that it may have been cultivated in the Amazon Basin 6000 years ago. There are well-attested traces of it in coastal Ecuador by 3400 years ago. Maize is, in fact, a peculiarly domesticated plant, dependent on humans for its very survival. The kernels are packed densely on the cob and if the cob was left to drop to the ground it would probably fail to germinate. Too many seedlings would be competing for space, light and nutrients, and so none would grow to maturity. Crossbreeding experiments have confirmed that maize in its modern form is the product of the hybridisation, some 4000 years ago, of a primitive cultivated maize with the wild perennial grass, teosinte.

All in all, the evidence suggests an agricultural evolution rather than a revolution, a notion supported by studies of stone-bladed sickles in the Middle East. Microscopic analysis of polish and wear indicates that the sickles were used to harvest cereals between 12 000 and 6000 years ago. Small-scale digging also took place 12 000 years ago. Over a period of thousands of years farming in the Middle East developed slowly, step by step, from being a small-scale affair to much larger-scale agricultural production.

FARMING CASE STUDY

The transition from hunter-gathering to full-scale agriculture was studied in detail at Abu Hureyra, a site on the banks of the Euphrates river in northern Syria. The site, excavated by archaeologists from Oxford, Cambridge and London Universities, was most probably that of an ancient village. It was inhabited on two occasions: first, by

hunter-gatherers from 11 500 to 10 000 years ago, during the Mesolithic period, when there were about 200-300 villagers; and later, about 9500 years ago, by Stone Age agriculturalists who numbered 2000 to 3000.

The site consists of a large mound, covering an area of around 28 acres (11.5 ha), created by the collapsed mud walls of the houses that once occupied it. Mixed in with the mud is a substantial collection of debris including animal bones and plant remains. The earlier Mesolithic villagers collected a wide range of wild seeds, including the wild forms of wheat, lentils, rye, barley, hackberries and pistachios. The later settlers cultivated domestic cereals, such as emmer, einkorn (another kind of wheat), oats, barley, chickpeas and lentils.

continued on page 118

The animal debris on the site revealed an interesting fact. Some 40 000 bones were uncovered and analysed, including those of onagers (a subspecies of wild ass, now found only in parts of north-western Iran), sheep, goats, pigs, deer and wild cattle. But these represented only a minority. A good 80 per cent of the bones were from animals that we know did not inhabit the river valley at all, since valleys are not their natural habitat. Indeed, the largest number of them came from the Persian or goitered gazelle, now almost extinct in the Middle East, which then lived on the nearby steppe.

The climate of the area was more or less the same as it is today. About 8 in (200 mm) of rain falls each year, placing the area just inside the zone where no irrigation is needed. The animals other than the gazelles would have thrived here – that is, until mankind slaughtered them and the local hunters were forced to find the bulk of their animal protein out on the steppe. The gazelles, adapted to arid conditions, thrived on the steppe without large quantities of leaves and water. The animals were also seasonally plentiful as they passed near to the

settlement during their annual spring and autumn migrations.

The hunting techniques were sophisticated. The hunters did not target a single animal, usually a young male which can be easily separated from the herd, and then kill it. Instead, they took on an entire herd at one time. Evidence for this came from the

ANCIENT GOURMET

Scientists in Germany have analysed the baked-in residues on cooking pots and been able to work out what foods ancient chefs prepared. They examined shards of Stone Age pots, reckoned to be more than 5000 years old, that were unearthed near Lake Geneva and found traces of fish fat and mustard-seed oil. Curiously, whitefish in mustard sauce is a popular delicacy in Swiss households and restaurants today.

gazelles' teeth. They showed that the victims were from all ages and both sexes. The presence of very young gazelles amongst the bone debris also suggests that all the preg-

CATTLE INSPECTION *An Egyptian wall painting shows domestic cattle been examined, perhaps before market. Opposite: Middle Eastern villagers drive wild gazelle into a 'desert kite'.*

nant females in the herd had recently given birth, an event which occurs in modern times in April and May. The hunt, therefore, must have taken place each year in early summer.

The mass killing was well-planned using permanent traps built on the steppe. These traps, which are found throughout the Middle East, are known as 'desert kites' on account of their shape: from the air they resemble a kite. Each one consists of two very long walls made from piles of stones or stone slabs set on their edge which extend out onto the steppe for a couple of miles. These 'training walls' are formed into a V-shape and they converge on the narrow entrance to a huge stone enclosure that can measure up to 500 ft (150 m) across.

The open end of the V-structure often stretched out near a stream at the entrance

WILD SHEEP *The Soay sheep is a primitive breed that has returned to its wild state on the Scottish island of St Kilda.*

to a valley; the hunters would have chosen valleys that the herds passed through on their way north each spring. The gazelles were stampeded into the killing enclosure at the other end, which was often positioned just over the brow of a hill to hide the waiting hunters. Depending on the terrain and available building materials, there were rock-lined emplacements containing archers with bows and arrows or pitfalls into which the fleeing animals fell. These were positioned at intervals around the periphery of the enclosure. The animals were killed and eaten. It is even possible that the meat might have been salted and dried, in which case it would have been available for consumption throughout the year.

Desert kites were discovered in the late 1920s when the first regular airline routes were being opened up. A pilot on the Cairo to Baghdad run wrote up the first account in 1929, but interpreted the stone patterns as defence structures. Later it became clear what they were really intended for: as a hunting device that the Plains Indians of North America also

employed when they drove herds of buffalo and pronghorn antelope over cliffs and into concealed pitfalls.

THE SHEEP AND THE GOATS
Of the other bones found at Abu Hureyra, the sheep and goat remains are also of interest. Wild sheep and goats tend to live at higher altitudes, and so the chances are that ones at a lowland site were domesticated. There are comparatively few of their bones in the more ancient settlement but they appear in larger numbers in the later one. A few domesticated sheep and goats, however, would not have satisfied the needs of the community.

The conclusion reached by archaeologists is that the Stone-Age people of Abu Hureyra were sustained by seasonal mass killings of gazelles, topped up with some domesticated animals and primitive crops. Domestication and arable farming were not self-evidently superior to the old hunter-gatherer ways, and there was no sudden shift from one system to the other. Instead, it seems that the two methods of obtaining food ran in parallel for up to 1000 years.

Then, about 8500 years ago, things changed dramatically: gazelles accounted for only 20 per cent of the meat consumed at the site and the slaughter of domestic animals increased to 80 per cent. It may be that the appearance of many more desert kites to the south meant that other communities were siphoning off the gazelles, intercepting them at an earlier point in their migration. In northern Jordan kites overlap in great chains across the plains. The herds were probably decimated, and the people of Abu Hureyra had to turn to agriculture to survive.

SECRETS OF EVERYDAY LIFE
The Abu Hureyra site not only provided scientists with information about hunting and farming, but also offered insights into the way its people went about their everyday lives. These secrets were revealed by the human bones found there, particularly those of the women.

Bones can give us information about diseases and also about the way people worked. The stresses and strains of regularly carrying heavy loads, for example, can be seen in bones. Studies of the vertebrae of young people from Abu Hureyra who died during their adolescence show that they carried loads on their heads. Experts have speculated that their tasks may have included

PRECIOUS PORK *Pigs were one of the first animals to be domesticated in South-east Asia, and today in Indonesia they are carefully looked after.*

carrying meat, baskets of grain and building materials.

One thing that puzzled scientists was the frequency amongst women of a collapsed last dorsal vertebra and an arthritic big toe. The women also showed signs of having muscular arms and legs. Many had strained knee joints. The injuries suggested an activity that had something to do with kneeling. Further excavations uncovered rubbing stones and 'saddle querns'. These are saddle-shaped mill stones for grinding grain by hand, and they were probably used in the kneeling position.

Plant seeds that had been collected or cultivated needed considerable preparation before they could be consumed, and this daily toil is evident in the bones. The saddle quern was placed on the floor and the woman knelt in front of it. Grain was placed on the upper surface of the quern and the rubbing stone scraped back and forth over it. The woman used both hands repeatedly to push the rubbing stone away and pull it

GRINDING GRAIN *Bronze Age trough querns for grinding grain, found on the Shetland Islands, have been worn away by the rounded pestle-like 'moulers'. Overleaf: Made of lapis lazuli and inlaid shell, this scene showing men with goats and cattle was found at Ur and is dated about 2600 BC.*

back, an activity that occupied many hours a day. Her bones – particularly in the back, knee and big toe, which was curled forward – showed the stresses it entailed, the repetitive stress syndrome of the Stone Age. It was a method of grinding which was common in desert regions until recent times.

Women's teeth also showed deformities. Grooves on the front teeth were found to be identical to those on the teeth of modern Paiute Indian women in North America. They acquire the grooves when basket-weaving. In the case of the Abu Hureyra women, three strands of plant material were needed for weaving, two

manipulated with the hands while the third was held in the teeth, wearing down the grooves in the front teeth. Evidence of this kind of wear and tear came from a particular part of the village and not elsewhere, suggesting that there were craft areas where a few specialists made products for the entire community.

In another of Abu Hureyra's craft areas, jaws had enlarged surfaces to the joints, suggesting heavy usage, and an uneven pattern of wear on the teeth. A similar configuration has been seen in recent times in the teeth and jaws of Maoris in New Zealand. It was caused by chewing plant stems to produce fibres for rope and mats. Impressions of mats were found in the mud at Abu Hureyra.

By 7500 years ago, different people in Abu Hureyra were taking on a greater variety of different roles than is usual in hunter-gatherer communities. Women were *continued on page 124*

CEREAL CULTIVATION *Still being grown today in Israel, emmer wheat (left) was cultivated in the Middle East about 10 000 years ago. Dating from the time of Egypt's 5th Dynasty, the wall chart (below) depicts intensive cereal cultivation in the Nile Valley.*

NEOLITHIC BOWL *A painted pottery bowl, dated 4000 BC, was found in the ruins of the farming village Pan-p'o in northern China.*

occupied with things around the home, while the men went hunting, developed animal husbandry and cultivated crops. New skills were becoming necessary, too. Agriculture demanded water and so irrigation was necessary. Animals had to be kept away from the crops lest they eat them. Harvested grain had to be transported from the fields to the village. Pottery was being made by about 7300 years ago, and baskets, mats, fences and the skills to make them were similarly being devised.

FARMING PROS AND CONS

By studying the people of Abu Hureyra and other early farmers in different parts of the world, archaeologists have been able to observe their transition from hunter-gatherers to agriculturalists. They are also able to observe the effects of farming on mankind.

Generally speaking, hunter-gatherers had more free time than early farmers tied to the yearly round of tilling and harvesting. On the other hand, farmers did not have to move around in pursuit of prey to hunt or to gather wild crops. Their communities were more stable; they were able to have larger families.

There were other advantages, too. When, about 7300 years ago, the craftswomen of Abu Hureyra developed pottery it allowed them to soak cereals and cook them as a kind of porridge. Women were able to feed their youngsters porridge and wean them off milk at an earlier age. Better nourishment and early weaning resulted in increased fertility. The interval between births would have been reduced and the village would have expanded more rapidly.

On the down side, agriculture led people to live together in crowded communities which began to trade with similarly crowded societies elsewhere. Conditions were ripe for diseases to pass from one society to the next and epidemics spread quickly. One result was high child mortal-ity rates, which offset the advantages of greater fertility.

MILKING TIME IN EGYPT
A cow has its back legs hobbled while it is being milked in this scene from an Egyptian relief.

The skeletons of children at Abu Hureyra show a thickening and pitting of the eye sockets indicating that they suffered from anaemia following a prolonged infestation by parasites. Dental caries also made its appearance, since cooked foods tend to stick to the teeth more than wild, unprocessed foods, providing a base for bacteria to grow.

Elsewhere in the world, archaeologists have found evidence of other drawbacks. Prehistoric hunter-gatherers, for instance, had an average height of 5 ft 9 in (175 cm) for men and 5 ft 5 in (165 cm) for women, but by 5000 years ago the averages were 5 ft 3 in (160 cm) for men and only 5 ft (152 cm) for women. Preagricultural people had a life expectancy of 26 years; afterwards they were lucky to reach 19. Falling life expectancy might have been a result, among other things, of a less varied diet.

Hunter-gatherers had (and have) an extremely varied diet, whereas farming communities concentrate on a few starch-rich crops. Modern Bushmen select from more than 75 wild plants, while modern urbanised people rely mainly on just five high-carbohydrate plants – wheat, rice, sorghum, millet and maize – each one lacking vital vitamins essential for a healthy life. Hunter-gatherers can also find alternatives if one plant is in short supply, whereas farmers may starve if their crop fails – witness, in relatively recent times, the failure of the Irish potato crop in 1845 and 1846.

Agriculture also brought divisions in society. It was probably responsible for the phenomenon of 'class'. Hunter-gatherers acquired what they needed day-by-day, but agriculture and the storing of foods meant that some people could live off the labour of others. The concept of kings, aristocracy, middle and working classes arose. There was a healthy, nonproducing elite who could separate themselves in some measure from the disease-ridden masses. At the same time, women produced more babies more often, in order to produce more hands to labour in the fields – this inevitably meant a certain loss of freedom for women. Agriculture supported a larger number of people, but it could be said that they 'enjoyed' a poorer quality of life than their hunter-gatherer predecessors.

It used to be argued that war was a by-product of agriculture, a natural progression from the notion of possessions and land ownership. This has been disproved, however. Rock art, about 10 000 years old, was discovered in Arnhem Land in northern Australia which reveals battle scenes considered to be the oldest-known depictions of conflict. They show humans spearing each other, hurling boomerangs,

dodging spears and chasing about with raised weapons. Some figures are shown with spears piercing them, while others have people bending over stricken comrades.

These early skirmishes involved small bands of fighters, but by 6000 years ago Aboriginal rock art shows many more warriors in large battles using relatively modern weapons, such as spear-throwers and three-pronged spears. The leaders in these battles wear suitably large and elaborate headdresses.

The increasing scale of such conflicts seems to run parallel with a crisis at the end of the Ice Age when sea levels rose and parts of Arnhem Land were flooded. The inhabitants – hunter-gatherers – were forced to share less land and less food, and tended

WELL WATER *In dry conditions water for people and domestic stock must be drawn up from a well.*

to fight.

In Europe, meanwhile, increasing conflict does seem to have been associated with agriculture. Britons are thought to have gone to war first about 6000 years ago, at a time when cattle breeding was on the increase. Some experts have suggested that cattle were becoming a measure of tribal wealth and thus a focus of conflict. Rustling was rife because the animals were so easy to steal and move about the country. Pigs, by contrast, were more difficult because they tended to return 'home' like dogs and homing pigeons. Sheep were also difficult to move around because they scattered in all directions – the flocking urge has been bred into them since ancient times. This first period of warring between rival groups and communities ended about 5000 years ago when the early prehistoric states emerged. A period of relative stability followed when the great monuments of Avebury, Stonehenge and Silbury Hill were built.

HORSES, DOGS AND WHEELS

Not all animals that humans domesticated were used for food. The wolf was domesticated to guard the sheep that it normally attacked, and the horse was harnessed as transport, a task made easier once mankind had invented the wheel.

Why did people first take wild animals into captivity and breed from them? Some authorities have suggested that animal horns, such as those of sheep, goats and cattle, had a religious significance: they resembled the curve of a sickle-shaped moon, worshipped in many ancient societies. One expert has proposed that herbivores were initially rounded up to prevent them eating the crops of arable farmers. Mankind had hunted such creatures for tens of thousands of years. It may

have occurred to the farmers that rounded them up that they should keep them in captivity, thus ensuring a dependable supply of live food as an insurance against hard times.

Climatic change may have played a role. Some places became warmer and wetter after the Ice Age, while others turned downright hot and dry. Humans and animals in arid regions would inevitably have congregated around waterholes and other sources of water. Mankind seized the opportunity and captured the wild animals.

Why goats, sheep, pigs and cattle were domesticated and not deer, gazelles and antelope, all of which were available to Stone Age people, is unclear. Deer and antelope have a strong territorial sense, which may have caused problems for early stock-keepers – it might have made things difficult when trying to move herds of them from place to place. The traditional farm animals are easy to herd, confine and move around even in their

wild state. Yet despite their territorial sense, deer such as red deer have taken readily to domestication on modern farms in northern Europe, and many ornamental parks have been stocked with species such as Père David's deer both in Europe and the Far East throughout history.

TAMING THE WOLF

Mankind probably tamed all sorts of mammals, keeping the young in captivity until they were too big, too boisterous or too savage to stay. The ones that remained close to people were most likely the social animals – ones that tend to form packs – and a creature that took to domestication especially readily was the wolf. Some zoologists believe that the Etruscan wolf, a primitive species resembling the modern small wolf of India, was the common ancestor of both dogs and today's different species of wolf. It evolved about a million years ago and ranged throughout Eurasia for thousands of years. It was still in existence at the time that people and wolves formed a partnership.

The process of domestication might have started when these wolves scavenged at middens or garbage tips near human settlements. Here, there would have been plenty of hides and rotting flesh to eat. Some wolves were caught, maybe for food, and their pups may have been fattened up for the pot. The more docile individuals were allowed to stay. Alternatively, man might initially have seen the wolf as a competitor. Then, while trying to eliminate it, he may have thought of harnessing its ability to warn of danger and its prowess at hunting. Gradually, he began to depend on the wolf

MOON GODDESS *A female figure holds up the curved horn of a bison, possibly indicating that the carving represents a fertility goddess.*

COMPANIONS *At Ein Mallaha, northern Israel, a person has been found buried with a puppy or wolf cub.*

dog as companion and guardian, and the wolf dog in turn grew to depend on man for food and shelter and so joined his 'pack'.

Wolves, like the ancient peoples who first domesticated them, are cooperative hunters, living in social groups in which rules and regulations determine an individual's behaviour. The wolf amongst men was like a wolf in its pack, except that the pack leader was a person rather than an 'alpha' wolf – the dominant male in a wolf pack. Wolf cubs were 'imprinted' – the process by which baby animals form attachments to their mothers or, in certain circumstances, other animals or even objects during their first hours of life. Over the centuries, the dog became man's best friend, used for hunting and herding.

One of the clearest indications that man and dog wolf had become partners emerged in 1977 from an excavation at Ein Mallaha in the Hula Basin in northern Israel. French archaeologists working on the site, estimated to be between 12 000 and 11 000 years old, uncovered the grave of an old person. The sex was difficult to establish as the pelvis was damaged, but under his or her left hand was the skeleton of a puppy which had died at the age of about three to five months. The relationship appeared to be one of affection rather than gastronomy. It was the first evidence of a man-animal relationship.

It is not clear whether the animal was the puppy of a domesticated dog or a captured wolf cub, but jawbones of similar animals elsewhere on the site offer some clues.

The jaws and the teeth are smaller than those of a mature wolf, a trait that accompanied the domestication of wolves in other parts of the Middle East. This suggests that people kept domesticated dog wolves at Ein Mallaha and that the puppy was probably a domestic animal rather than a tamed wolf.

In the centuries that followed, the dog was often depicted in art and sculptures. Small statuettes of dogs with curled tails, dating from about 7500 years ago, were found in Iraq. Dog bones have been found at an excavation in Yorkshire, England, dating from even earlier, 9500 years ago. In

North America the remains of two sizes of dog were found at Jaguar Cave, Idaho, and were reckoned to be 10 300 years old.

Today, the dog has been specially bred into a great diversity of forms and, although it has retained many of its physical attributes, such as acute hearing and a keen sense of smell, it is a shadow of its former self. In reality, domestication, while making the dog more malleable, has reduced its ability to react to the pressures and stimuli encountered in the wild. The greyhound may run faster than the wolf, for instance, but its hearing and sense of smell are not nearly as good. On the other hand, many physical features have been bred in, some to enhance the abilities of working dogs, others with a more decorative intent. Breeding has been a way to create a wolf for every occasion. Pictures from ancient Mesopotamia show mastiffs bred for hunting lions and, later, in Egypt, long-legged greyhound-like dogs and short-legged terrier-like ones were depicted in tomb paintings.

Another aid to domestication was castration. The dog itself rarely suffered this fate, but the few surviving remains of male farm animals from the early Neolithic period suggest that many of them may have had their testes removed. It would have left them easier to tame and handle. Castrated bulls and stallions, for example, were good for hauling materials or farm implements such as ploughs. Castration before maturity also encouraged an animal to put on fat, producing valuable tallow for lamps and cooking after it was slaughtered.

THE HORSE REVOLUTION

The domestication of the horse was the first significant revolution in human land transport. It was once thought to have started about 4000 years ago – horses used by military cavalry appear in the rock art of that age. But evidence obtained during the past couple of decades indicates that the horse may have been domesticated far earlier. This includes the jaws of horses found in southern France in 1911, which show signs of 'crib biting' – the habit that captive horses (but never wild ones) have of biting a rail, rope or even rock when bored. The jaws were originally estimated to be 30 000 years old, though they were re-examined more recently and the estimated age modified to at least 12 000 years old.

The general feeling today is that humans had definitely domesticated horses and were riding them by about 6000 years ago. Confirming this is a site at Dereivka in Ukraine, dating from about that time, which contains the skull, lower jaw and forelimb bones of a mature horse. The seven or eight-year-old 'Dereivka stallion' was found buried alongside two dogs and several ceramic human figurines.

Researchers from Hartwick College in Oneonta, New York, were invited by the Ukraine Academy of Sciences to study the remains, and they made casts of the cheek teeth. Examination under an electron microscope revealed that the teeth were bevelled in front and had smooth, polished surfaces on the sides with small cracks in them. The pattern of tooth wear matched that in modern horses that have been ridden and was unlike that seen in wild horses. They concluded that the dental wear was

continued on page 132

THE HUNT *Assyrian huntsmen are shown with hounds in a relief carving at Ashurbanipal's Palace at Nineveh. Horses (overleaf) were highly prized by the Assyrians, who needed them in very large numbers for warfare, and in peacetime for hunting.*

INVENTING THE WHEEL

When the Sumerians of ancient Mesopotamia invented the wheel about 3500 BC, they first used it as a potter's wheel to shape cooking utensils. It was not used for transport until a few hundred years later.

The first wheels for transport were made of solid wood, and attached to carts. But the Sumerians did not make them in the obvious way – by taking a cross-section of a tree trunk. It must somehow have become clear to them that a simple section of tree has inherent weaknesses – the heart-wood and knots fall out and the wood cracks both along the lines of annual growth and along the so-called medullary rays, where side boughs once branched off. Instead they took three pieces of wood, cut lengthwise from a tree trunk and shaped them into a wheel. Two semicircular shapes were fastened by external wooden struts or internal dowels (round pins) to a central rectangular piece, thus forming a rough circle.

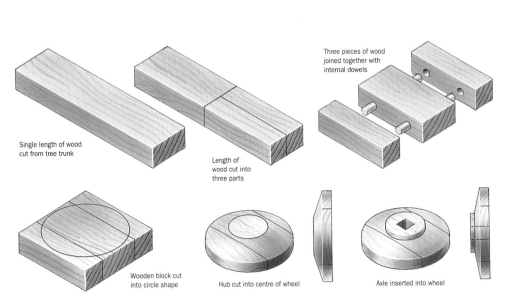

Single length of wood cut from tree trunk

Length of wood cut into three parts

Three pieces of wood joined together with internal dowels

Wooden block cut into circle shape

Hub cut into centre of wheel

Axle inserted into wheel

At its centre, they cut a hub in which the axle was inserted. The wheel was prevented from slipping off the rounded axle with wooden pegs or linchpins pushed through a perforation near its outer end.

Later, the wooden cross-struts were replaced by metal strips, and wooden felloes, or bands, with copper studs or complete copper bands were placed around the outside of the wheel to give it added strength and durability. Sections were then carved out of the solid wheel, in order to lighten the weight, and by about 200 BC spoked wheels had evolved.

Prehistoric solid wooden wheels have also been found in the Netherlands, dating from about 2500 BC, but the unseasoned wood, from which the wheel would have been honed, would have weighed $1/3$ ton (322 kg) and required a hardwood, oak, say, at least 150 years old. These elderly trees are not common, and so the early Dutch wheelwrights were forced, not only by structural considerations but also by the availability of wood to construct the lighter threepiece disc wheel.

At first, wheels were attached to simple flat sledges, but as wheeled transport developed the Sumerians constructed both two and four-wheeled carts with sides. These were

WAGON WHEELS *This model of a wagon, made of terracotta and dated 2000 BC, is from Syria.*

DISC WHEEL *The solid wheel cannot be made from a cross-section of tree trunk, but must be cut lengthways to avoid weaknesses in the wood.*

usually pulled by oxen or by onagers, a local species of wild ass. Axles were detachable. Outside the cities, roads must have been difficult to negotiate or non-existent, and so carts were dismantled and carried by hand or loaded onto oxen until flatter ground was found. The front axles could not swivel, making it difficult to turn corners. That development was not to appear for another 2000 years.

Nevertheless, the early wheeled cart was invaluable. It has been estimated that an ox or onager could have pulled in a cart three times as much as it would have carried on its back. And its military potential was quickly realised. Two-wheeled battle cars (chariots with solid wheels) and four-wheeled battle wagons, both drawn by onagers, are depicted on carvings on limestone slabs and in cuneiform signs on clay tablets. Covered wagons, with an arched tilt or awning of matting are shown in pictures and models dated between 2350 and 2100 BC.

NOBLE COMPANION *The elegant figure of a horse, immortalised in mammoth ivory, was found at Vogelherd in Germany.*

associated with a bit, probably a rope bit. Further evidence was found in the form of perforated antler tines (spikes), resembling cheek pieces through which reigns could have been passed. Not all the horses from the Ukrainian site had the same patterns. Some teeth found on garbage middens had

no signs of 'bit wear' and were probably from animals kept and slaughtered for food.

The Dereivka stallion and the other horses belonged to people from the Sredni Stog culture who flourished in small settlements between 6300 and 5500 years ago east of the Dnieper River. They were hunters who travelled up the river valleys to reach the Eurasian steppe. Riding horses would have given them a tremendous advantage over agricultural communities living nearby.

Indeed, the horse gave people who used it a previously unheard-of mobility. With it they could travel up to 80 miles (130 km) in a day, substantially more than they could cover on foot, and they could use it to carry loads of up to 200 lb (90 kg) at a time. Raiding, hunting or foraging parties were able to

patrol larger territories, enabling them to travel to places that before then had been out of reach. Riding horses also changed the face of war. Warriors on horseback were able to attack a neighbouring community and be away before the residents had time to fight back. Possession of horses also conveyed a degree of power and status to individual horse owners, influencing the structure of society.

For many centuries, such horsemen rode their mounts either bareback or with no more than a cloth or blanket to act as a saddle. One of the first pieces of evidence of the saddle more or less as we know it is a

INTO BATTLE *In a war picture on the sound box of a lyre from Ur, dated 2600 BC, onagers (wild asses) pull a chariot with solid wheels.*

4th-century BC vase from Chertomylk in Russia. It shows a horse with a saddle and straps hanging from the side. Horseshoes were in use by the 2nd century BC. They were introduced by the Scythians, descendants of the first horsemen of the Eurasian steppe.

The horse even has a bearing on the origins of the Indo-European languages, the vast family of tongues whose modern members range from English to Hindi, German to Romany (the language of the Gypsies), Italian to Russian. By Roman times, the forerunners of many of these tongues were already spoken from India to Europe. They had almost certainly replaced the more ancient languages of Europe of which Basque, Finnish, Estonian and Hungarian are today among the few survivors. The Indo-European languages still have a few words that resemble each other. Almost all of them relate to life not in agricultural communities but in societies where horses, wheeled transport and domesticated animals dominate. There are more such words associated with horses than with crops, for example. It has been suggested that the people who spoke the early Indo-European languages were the

THE FIRST PETS

The step from the domesticated animal as food or work assistant to the domesticated animal as intimate member of the household or family was not a long one. The ancient Andeans, for example, shared their homes with guinea pigs, which nibbled away at any morsels of dropped food (a useful hygienic measure) and themselves became food from time to time. Such relationships between man and beast could become positively tender. An Old Testament character from the time of King David, around 1000 BC, tells the story of a poor farmer who bought a ewe lamb: he 'nourished [it] up: and it grew up together with him, and with his children; it did eat of his own meat, and drank of his own cup, and lay in his bosom, and was unto him as a daughter'.

The wall paintings of the ancient Egyptians are evidence that they were animal lovers. They show pet monkeys, birds, dogs and, above all, cats. The process leading to the domestication of cats may have started in Egypt as early as 4000 BC. The native African wild cats, *Felis silvestris libyca*, were probably drawn to human settlements by grain stores with their populations of rats and mice. The Egyptians would have recognised the service rendered by cats in attacking the vermin, and might have encouraged them by leaving out food. Cat skeletons found in the cemeteries of predynastic Egypt (before 3050 BC) show that humans and cats were already living on intimate terms.

Other cultures were also taking to cats. Cretan wall tiles from about 1600 BC show hunting cats; the Greeks had domestic cats by the 5th century BC. Domestic cats appear in Chinese records by 500 BC and in Indian ones by 100 BC.

ANCIENT PETS *The mandibles of a domestic cat (top) from Cyprus, dated 6000 BC, and of a dog from Israel, dated 10 000 BC, show that these animals have been man's friends for thousands of years.*

each other. Almost all of them relate to life not in agricultural communities but in societies where horses, wheeled transport and domesticated animals dominate. There are more such words associated with horses than with crops, for example. It has been suggested that the people who spoke the early Indo-European languages were the

ANIMAL SEALS *A rhinoceros, elephant and local breed of cattle feature on signature seals, dated 2500 BC, from Mohenjo Daro in the Indus Valley, Pakistan.*

horsemen who rode onto the steppe from the Ukraine about 6000 years ago. They left their mark in a huge family of tongues spoken to this day.

In addition to the horse, other related equines were domesticated and bred to serve mankind. The wild ass was employed in North Africa, while the onager (a subspecies of wild ass) was tamed in central and south-west Asia. The ass is considered to be one of the oldest pack animals and was already in service in Egypt about 5500 years ago. Four onagers in yokes pulling a two-wheeled chariot – as well as oxen pulling two four-wheeled heavy carts – feature in Sumerian art from about 4600 years ago. The pictures were found in the royal tombs of Ur in Mesopotamia in 1927. The wheels of these ancient vehicles were made fast to their axles and so, when turning a corner, both wheels of a pair had to revolve at the same speed. One wheel would have skidded along the ground as the chariot or cart turned.

Of other draught animals, Asian elephants have been found on seals from the Indus Valley dating from 4500 years ago and a Chinese text of the 1st millennium BC describes reindeer being ridden. There is also indirect evidence, from around 400 BC, that reindeer may have been used to draw sledges at Pazyryk, north of the Altai Mountains on the borders of modern China, Russia and Mongolia. A chieftain there was buried with his sledge and horses. The horses wore reindeer masks, suggesting that reindeer, too, may have been used for such tasks.

VILLAGES, TOWNS AND CITIES

When people discovered places with a year-round food supply and stable physical conditions, they settled down. The resulting societies developed specialised skills in civil engineering, architecture, crafts and professions.

Fishermen probably established the first settlements. While the hunter's range would have been determined by the movements of the wandering herds that were his prey, the fisherman tended to keep to 'good ground'. Settlements grew up where fish and shellfish were plentiful and the fishing was good. One such site was Vaenget Nord, near the present-day town of Vedbaek to the north of Copenhagen. Today it is set back from the coast on dry land, but between about 7000 and 6800 years ago it was a small island in an inlet, separated from the mainland by a shallow, narrow channel. At that time the geography and climate of the region were undergoing rapid change.

The great ice sheets that covered Scandinavia, including Denmark, had receded and the newly emerging tundra landscape, with lichens and dwarf birches, was invaded by reindeer and hardy horses from the steppe. Human hunters from the south followed the game, but as the region warmed up and the vegetation changed to light forests of birch and pine, their prey changed, too. They started to hunt aurochs (an early species of cattle), moose, wild pigs, red deer and roe deer. The trouble was, there was not enough to sustain the populations of humans. Gradually the game died out in the region, partly perhaps as a result of overhunting, partly because of continuing changes in the climate and environment, and the hunters turned to the sea. In the Late Mesolithic Age (up to about 3700 BC), kitchen middens, the garbage tips of antiquity, started to appear all over Denmark. They contained the remains of fish and shellfish, such as oysters, mussels and scallops, and even the bones of porpoises and whales. The presence of the middens indicated that for part of each year at least the people were settling down, harvesting local waters.

THAMES PORT MEADOW *Sites such as this, on the bank of a shallow river, were typical places where early humans made their settlements.*

By about 7000 years ago Vaenget Nord was the site of a small camp. At that time the inhabitants had a choice of foods, including deer and wild pigs from the nearby forests on the mainland. But chemical analysis of human bones found at the site indicates that the local folk relied mainly on the sea for their food. This was determined by measuring the different isotopes of nitrogen. These depend on the sources of food people ate during their lives: red meat eaters tend to incorporate one isotope and fish eaters another. The Danish settlers had isotope levels equivalent to those found in Greenland Eskimos 75 per cent of whose diet, before the introduction of supermarkets, came from the sea.

THE SEA'S PLENTY

The sea was bountiful enough, providing enough food, to hold them back from taking up serious farming for several hundred years. It was fishing not farming that influenced them in establishing a settlement.

Its focus lay on the west side of the island, closest to the mainland. A depression in the ground today suggests that a large dwelling once stood there. The settlement was divided into different work areas: one where hides were worked, for example, and another where flint tools were made. There was a burial pit, and rubbish dumps to the north and south, one of which contains hazelnut shells – the nuts were widely eaten throughout Europe at that time. The remains of fish, such as gar, mackerel, dogfish and stingray, were also found. And there was a cemetery.

The cemetery is thought to be about 6000 years old. It contained the graves of 22 people, including eight adult males, eight adult females and five infants. Adult males were buried with their working implements, such as flint knives; females were buried with jewellery made from shells and the teeth of aurochs, bears and moose. Some of these animals were extinct in the region at the time, and so there must have been trade with communities farther south in Europe. One infant was buried on a swan's wing next to an adult female who is presumed to be his mother.

Vaenget Nord was probably occupied for most of the year, but not all of it. The presence of hazelnuts, which ripen in autumn, and fish, which are more readily caught in spring and summer, suggests that the inhabitants stayed there for the warmer months, much as modern Scandinavians head in summer for their seaside homes. Its was the focus of activities that ranged from hunting and fishing to butchering and skinning. In the cold, wet, windy winters the fishermen headed for more sheltered mainland sites along the inlet.

Vaenget Nord was by no means the only settlement in the area. Archaeologists have discovered 40 or more village sites round about, indicating that the fishing was very good. People lived around the inlet from about 7200 years ago, not long after it was formed, until 5200 years ago when the gradual introduction of agriculture started very slowly to change the previous patterns of life in the region.

VAENGET NORD *Archaeologists have uncovered evidence that has allowed them to build up a detailed picture of life in the 7000-year-old settlement.*

Other changes, too, were afoot. Sea levels were rising, due to the melting of the ice sheets, and eventually submerged the island of Vaenget Nord. This robbed its people of their home, but it also created a rich fishing bank. The remains of a 5700-year-old dugout canoe were found there, suggesting that fishermen from the mainland and from islands not engulfed by the sea regularly visited it. When the weight of ice was finally removed from the region, northern Denmark, along with the rest of Scandinavia, started to rise out of the sea again, a process that continues, albeit more slowly, today. Vaenget Nord is now high and dry once more, and archaeologists are slowly peeling away its secrets.

In other parts of the world, different influences encouraged mankind to settle down. One direct consequence of agriculture and of the domestication of animals was the concentration of people into small, permanent settlements. The hunter, trapper and scavenger became the Neolithic farmer and herdsman. Growing crops meant that people were forced to stay in one place for at least as long as the crop was growing. They had to tend it, keep animals from eating it and eventually harvest it.

A Stone Age family gathering a normal family-sized harvest over three weeks could store away about a ton of grain, enough to keep them going for around a year. This grain had to be stored in secure structures which needed to be constructed, maintained and protected, further factors tying them to a more permanent home.

Another means of storage was the domesticated animal itself. Ancient man not only had fresh meat available 'on the hoof', but he could also rely on the ability of animals, particularly mammals, to put on fat when times were good and use that fat when times were hard. Camels have a fat-filled hump, for example, and fat-tailed sheep, as their name suggests, store fat in the tail. Pigs spread out the fat below the thick skin, while mountain sheep lay down fat around the kidneys. Eating fat is not the most efficient way of getting energy, but it was useful as a standby. Factors like these enabled people to remain and survive in one locality, even when conditions there were unfavourable.

FIRST CITY *An aerial view (below) and a reconstruction (left) of Mohenjo Daro, which rose to prominence in 2400 BC, shows that the city was based on a grid system, like New York. It was the largest of about 100 towns in the Indus Valley at that time.*

Farming also enabled a greater number of people to live together than hunting and foraging did. Inevitably, the size of a community depended on the productivity of the land around, but trade and transport as they developed helped to reduce that dependence. They enabled people to move food from where it was produced to where it was needed. This development in turn called for market places, another kind of permanent site. Temporary shelters such as tents would have been inappropriate for stores, markets and village homes and so constructions became more durable, their materials extending to wood, mud, reeds and straw.

Some of the first inland settlements were in the Near East. A site that may be as much as 11 000 years old at Zawi Chemi Shanidar in northern Iraq consists of oval, semipermanent huts. Found on the same site were heavy-duty axe blades and the remains of wild sheep. At the same time, artefacts fashioned from native copper were appearing at hill sites at Çayönü Tepesi and Çatal Hüyük in Turkey and Ali Kosh in Iran. The coppersmiths obtained their metal from veins near to settlements and shaped it by cold hammering. At first it was probably used for decoration but it soon began to appear in tools. By 9000 years ago or a little after there is evidence from Turkey of ore smelting, although it was not to appear in Iran until more than 2500 years later.

URBAN LIVING IN THE INDUS VALLEY

Settlements became villages and these grew into towns. Eventually cities were built. About 4500 years ago some of the first cities – notably Mohenjo Daro – emerged in the Indus Valley of what is now Pakistan. Some contained upwards of 40 000 inhabitants, and were in existence at around the same time as the great cities of Mesopotamia. Evidence includes that from excavations made by French archaeologists at Mehrgarh. This shows that a large village of 15 acres (6 ha) stood there in 7000 BC, and a small town of 30 acres (12 ha) with a population of 3000 by 6000 BC.

Pottery figures, including 20 unbaked clay figurines of women, and the remains of

water containers made from straw baskets that had been coated with bitumen have also been unearthed at Mehrgarh. By 6000 BC the inhabitants were producing crude pottery effigies of bulls and women, and 1500 years later they had learned to make sophisticated wheel-thrown painted ceramics.

continued on page 140

CITY STREET *Straight, parallel streets in Mohenjo Daro were lined with buildings made of weather-resistant, fired bricks. The trench in the foreground (overleaf) is part of the well-maintained sewage system at Mohenjo Daro.*

HOUSE RECONSTRUCTION
*Many early houses were made
of wattle and daub, with mud
thrown over a framework of
sticks or reeds.*

The town itself was rather
utilitarian, with houses and
granaries but no palaces or
temples. Nearby Naushaharo,
which covered a 30 acre (12 ha)
site, was more sophisticated.
Town walls that were 35 ft (10 m)
thick and 15 ft (4.6 m) high
have been discovered, and in its
centre a circular brick building
containing human figurines is
thought to be a temple.

The Indus Valley's largest
urban site of all can safely be described as a
'city'. The 150 acre (60 ha) site of Mohenjo
Daro, 200 miles (320 km) north of modern
Karachi, has wide streets with
mud-brick buildings,

RICH AND FAMOUS *Wealth
brought status. A rich man
would have owned many
treasures, including
statuettes of himself.*

and was recently found to extend a mile
(1.6 km) farther to the east than previously
thought. In its heyday Mohenjo Daro was
probably the largest city in the world with a
population of 40 000 people or more. Cities
had come to stay, and in other parts of
the world they would emerge wherever societies grew in wealth and
sophistication – from Zhengzhou,
capital of Shang-dynasty China,
founded around 1700 BC; to
Teotihuacán in modern Mexico
with an estimated population of
200 000 people by AD 500; and
the trading metropolis of Great
Zimbabwe in southern Africa,
spreading over a 100 acre (40 ha)
site from the 10th century AD until
its decline 500 years later.

THE FIRST NATION-STATE

In Egypt 6000 years ago farming
towns arose along the course of
the Nile river. The river itself
became an artery of trade that
linked the Lower Nile settlements at the mouth of the river

with the Upper Nile towns farther south.
The area is of special interest, because it has
revealed a number of clues about the way
nation-states emerged.

Gradually, one or two major cities grew
up as centres of industry, trade and political
power. One such city, 5800 to 5300 years
ago, was Hierakonpolis or 'City of the Fal-
cons', as it was known to the Greeks, or
Nekhen, as it was known to the ancient predynastic Egyptians. It was situated in Upper
Egypt on a protected rise in the Nile flood-
plain. It had houses, crafts areas and rubbish
tips, and around the town were small farming communities and cemeteries. During a
period of 500 years the population grew from
several hundred to an estimated 10 500
people living in a variety of dwellings.

Out in the country, herders and some
farmers had semi-permanent, seasonal huts,
but the dwellers of the town itself and the
surrounding villages had more permanent
buildings. The less permanent homes were
round huts, whereas the more robust ones
were rectangular, built of mud-brick or
wattle-and-daub. Wattle-and-daub buildings
consisted of a framework of interwoven strips
of wood and reeds over which mud was plastered. The floors were sometimes sunk several inches below ground level. Some of the
houses were positioned close together and
surrounded by fences, and artefacts found
scattered amongst them indicate that a few

PARLOUR GAMES *Part of a chessboard found at Mohenjo Daro suggests that the idle rich had time to invent and play games.*

the mountains. The wind, acting like a kind of natural bellows, fanned the flames to the temperatures required to fire the higher-quality pots and jars.

Another local industry was the manufacture of maceheads. Indeed, by far the most exciting find in one of the larger tombs was a finished macehead. It was disc-shaped and made of polished porphyry, a medium to fine-grained igneous rock. It would have been the possession of an ancient nobleman or man of substance, a member of the group of rulers

ever as the capital of a kingdom that encompassed most of Upper Egypt – a similar process in the north had resulted in a kingdom of Lower Egypt ruled from Buto in the Nile Delta.

By 5100 years ago, Hierakonpolis's rulers had conquered all Egypt, and their leader Narmer, from the Egyptian word for 'catfish', was the most powerful political figure in the Middle East. He was given the name Menes and became the first pharaoh and the

BUILDING BLOCKS *From earliest times bricks made from mud were used for buildings intended to be permanent. Later, stone was used, as at the site of Great Zimbabwe in Zimbabwe, which dates from AD 1200 (overleaf).*

house owners had a higher status in society than others.

Excavations of the cemeteries have revealed information about the town's elite. They were not buried in ordinary graves; instead, they were placed in large, rectangular tombs placed apart from the tombs of lesser mortals. By the time the archaeologists had found them they had been looted, but nevertheless enough artefacts survived to be able to assess the status of the dead person who had been buried there. There were the remains of baskets, braided leather rope, painted arrow shafts, flint arrowheads, grass matting and pieces of the wooden trestle on which a coffin had been placed. There were also fragments of painted papyrus-like parchment and pottery with what appeared to be writing on it. These finds prompted the researchers to suggest that Egyptian writing was far older than was once thought.

In one tomb was a black-topped clay jar in the style known to archaeologists as Plum Red Ware. It was a product of the principal industry in and around Hierakonpolis and the reason for the region's wealth. The city was the centre of a thriving industry producing two kinds of pottery: the Plum Red Ware, found in tombs, and Straw-tempered Ware, which was used for everyday purposes. Fifteen kilns have been found in the area, those making the Plum Red Ware located high on desert cliffs. Here the kilns were positioned in such a way that they took advantage of breezes which blew through

of the city known as the 'Divine Souls of Nekhen'. They were the barons who controlled the city's potteries, trade and wealth.

By 5200 years ago the climate had changed and the region became drier. The pottery industry collapsed and the city moved closer to the Nile. The smaller barons invested their wealth in other industries and went to war with one another. At the end of 100 years of civil strife, however, Hierakonpolis emerged more powerful than

founder of the first dynasty. One side of a piece of carved slate, about 25 in (64 cm) high, depicts him wearing the white crown that had become the symbol of office of the ruler of Upper Egypt, on the other side he wears the red crown of Lower Egypt. The slate represents the unification of Egypt, the first nation-state. The pottery traders who had built up their wealth in predynastic times were the forefathers of the divine kings who ruled for thousands of years.

RITUAL, WORSHIP AND MONUMENT BUILDING

Fearful of the unknown and faced with the mysterious vagaries of life and death, people turned to the supernatural to explain the forces that shape existence. For inspiration, they looked to the 'life-giving' Sun, the Moon and the stars.

Neanderthals and early modern humans were almost certainly the first people to bury their dead, more than 100 000 years ago. Bodies have been found interred along with animal bones, suggesting that those still alive felt some kind of concern for the person who had died. Death rites had arrived and would remain a focus in the life of communities for many thousands of years to come.

Long before that, beginning in the early Palaeolithic period about 300 000 years ago, there is some evidence that the veneration of animal skulls may have been an important ritual for early man and his immediate forebears. At Regoundou in France, the huge, carefully buried skulls of ancient cave bears have been discovered, dating from about 40 000 years ago. The skulls of humans may have been similarly venerated in some places. There does not seem to have been anything cannibalistic about this; the skulls were probably cleaned and prepared long after the death of their owners.

Animal skulls may have been worshipped to bring good luck while hunting – a kind of magic exemplified by the cult of the cave bear, as at Regoundou, between 50 000 and 30 000 years ago – whereas a human skull might have been linked to heroic individuals.

BOG MEN

One aspect of the life of prehistoric modern man in northern Europe was the custom of dumping people in peat bogs as part of a fertility rite. The cult is thought to have arisen in a number of places – some experts believe that it was practised in what is now Denmark, in particular, as early as about 5500 years ago. This was a time when hunter-gathering was being replaced by agriculture and people all across northern Europe were beginning to gather into permanent settlements. The cult seems to have taken a particular hold in Denmark where it was practised until about AD 200 during the Viking age.

Its victims ranged considerably in age from a girl of 14 years old to a man of about 50 or 60, and their remains have been found throughout the region. These include Tollund Man from central Jutland in Den-

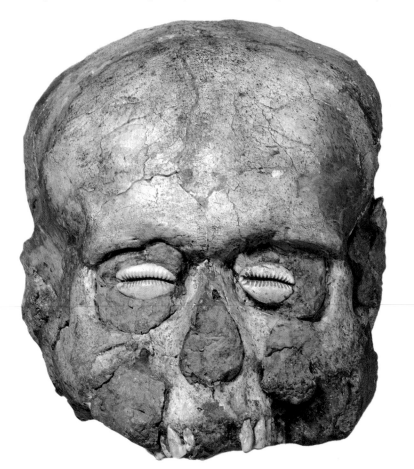

ICON *A female skull, found at Jericho dates back some 8000-7000 years. It has features modelled in plaster and cowrie-shell eyes, and was probably used during rituals.*

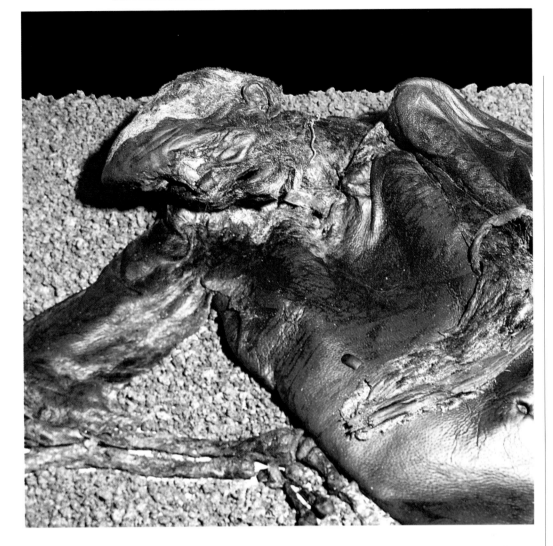

LINDOW MAN *The remains of an ancient human body, found in a peat bog in northern England, are those of a man who was ritually murdered.*

mark and Lindow Man from Cheshire, England. Some scholars believe that the Danish bog victims were sacrificed to the Nordic fertility gods Frej and Freja. In many cases, however, there may have been other explanations in Denmark and elsewhere. Some bog people may simply have got lost and sucked into the bog; others may have been executed. One Danish victim, for example, aged about 35 years old and severely crippled with a hip injury, had a piece of plaited rope around his neck, which suggests that he was hanged.

The Cheshire bog man is thought to have met his end as part of a Celtic 'rite of spring' ritual. Mistletoe pollen found in his gut indicates that he was a sacrificial victim – in later Druidic times mistletoe was frequently used in such rites. He is, in fact, one of the later bog victims, estimated to have been sacrificed about 2500 years ago. He was found in 1984 by a peat cutter who first alerted the police. They were soon replaced by archaeologists when people realised just how old the corpse was.

The man was in his mid-twenties. He was about 5 ft 6 in (1.7 m) tall, and he had ginger-coloured hair and a beard. His face appeared to be twisted with pain, and it was bent forwards onto his right shoulder. Around his neck was a thong made from animal sinew, which had been twisted from behind using a stick, cutting into his throat and cracking his vertebrae. He had been garrotted, after which he was thrown face down in a shallow pool in the peat bog.

He was discovered buried below several layers of peat, and so is well preserved. Normally, moulds and bacteria break down bod-

ies quickly, but the dark, acidic conditions in the bog preserved the body. This was helped by humic acid, a weak acid made from carbon dioxide dissolved in rain water, which pickled the body, and tannins from the peat which turned the skin to leather. Experts have not yet discovered why the Lindow Bog Man was chosen as a sacrifice, but one thing is sure: he was of high social standing. The manicured finger nails show that he was not accustomed to manual work.

ANIMAL SACRIFICES

Butchering tools that had been used on both animal and human bones have also been found. The bones seem to have been deliberately discarded in the same pits inside a cave. A few scholars regard this as evidence that people were eating other people, maybe as food, maybe in some kind of ritual, and then discarding their bones with the remains of other food.

These finds were made in the Fontbre-

goua cave in south-eastern France, and were estimated to be about 7000 years old. The cave itself, which was used from time to time as a camp 7000 to 6000 years ago, consisted of three chambers: a porch, a main room and a lower room. Pottery, stone tools, wild and domestic varieties of wheat and barley and the remains of humans have been found there. One pit has a circle of stones surrounding a domestic ox skull, while another contains the broken bones of six humans, including two children, together with the pieces of two stone bracelets and a small axe which is thought to have been used to butcher the bodies. The skulls, shoulder blades and some leg bones are missing. The rest of the bones have been broken to obtain the marrow, and they show marks of skinning, filleting and dismembering by stone implements.

Eight other pits in the cave contain the remains of butchered animals, including sheep and wild boar, but here again some of

WHEN A STAR EXPLODES

Astronomers believe that 6000 years ago a supernova (exploding star) positioned a comparatively modest 1300 light years away may have been the closest starburst witnessed by man. The Sumerians of ancient Mesopotamia, who saw it and wrote about it in cuneiform symbols on clay tablets, thought that a god had visited them on Earth. According to Mesopotamian legend, it was this event that sowed the seeds of civilisation. In the years that followed the star's explosion, the people of Sumer developed the wheel, created a written language, established the science of astronomy and foundations of mathematics, created a law code, provided the first school system, the first parliament and the first directory of medicines. Was it coincidence, or did the celestial event influence this episode in the story of mankind?

The star would have been seen in the southern sky, where the modern constellation of Vela borders that of Puppis. It was so bright that it became a second sun by day and was brighter than the moon at night. It waxed and then waned at the end of its life, first producing a gigantic stellar explosion and then receding into celestial oblivion as a pulsar, a collapsed star that emits pulses of energy mainly as radio waves.

That a star was evident at all was first mooted in 1912 when a tablet, thought to be an ancient catalogue of stars, was found in Mesopotamia. A giant star-like feature was recorded but when modern astronomers came to look for the star they could not find it. Then, in 1968, an Australian radio-telescope rediscovered the much reduced Sumerian star. It was spinning at 11 times a second on its axis, and emitting radio waves that could be picked up on Earth. Visual telescopes have since detected very indistinct flashes from it and have described it as one of the faintest objects in the sky. They gave it the unimaginative name PRS 0833-45 or Vela X.

The Sumerians were more impressed with Vela X; it has even been suggested by a few scholars that the desire to record the visit of this 'god' for posterity may have been

the stimulus for the origins of writing. It may also have stimulated an interest in astronomy and the desire in general to record the appearance, movement and position of heavenly bodies in the sky. The supernova would have been the talking point of every living person in Sumer, and it

WRITING TABLET *This clay tablet with star signs and other symbols is from Jamdat Nasr, Sumer, and dated 2800 BC.*

is perhaps significant that the first symbol in Sumerian script was a star, one of the first written words.

---

the lower leg bones and the shoulder blades are missing. Animals and humans were evidently butchered in the same way, leading some of the French archaeologists who excavated the site to suggest that the findings may be evidence of Neolithic cannibalism.

EARLY RELIGION

The Cantabrian caves of El Juyo, on the Atlantic coast of Spain, have structures on which burned offerings may have been made. There are also piles of deliberately discarded but perfectly good tools and weapons, and what appears to be a large sculpted and engraved rock that may represent a part-human and part-animal face.

Wild game was important in ancient Cantabrian life. A rich variety of animals enabled the people living at El Juyo and the surrounding region to eat well. There were ibex and chamois in the hills, wild boar, red deer and roe deer in the forests, bison, horses and aurochs in the meadows, salmon and trout in the streams, and fish and shellfish along the coast. Even during the Ice Age, mammoths, mastodons, reindeer, aurochs and horses sustained the people well. At El Juyo itself the dominant game was red deer, but salmon from streams and shellfish from the coast appear to have been on the menu, too.

El Juyo was about 200 ft (60 m) above sea level and about 3 miles (5 km) from the coast. The cave site contained some unusual structures, including a big oval-shaped depression, about 9 ft (3 m) long and 7 ft (2 m) wide, in the centre of which was a large pile of red deer bones. It was surrounded by a low wall of earth and stones that had been brought in from outside. Its function is unknown, but silts accumulated in its bottom suggest that at some time it was filled with water. Whether this was a means of preserving meat for the future or a way to dispose of leftovers in a kind of waste-disposal tank is far from clear. Nearby was a small dugout chamber whose purpose seemed to be clearer, as a store for grindstones, ochre, different coloured clays and partly carved deer antlers.

About 14 000 years ago the caves at El Juyo were blocked by rock falls and, save for a few Bronze Age and Roman explorations of the site, the inside of the caves remained in pristine condition until 1953 when Spanish and American archaeologists began to explore them. Their excavations opened the way to further remarkable discoveries.

They found a walled enclosure containing three trenches 8 in (20 cm) deep – one 30 in (76 cm) long, another 54 in (1.3 m) long and the third 60 in (1.5 m) long – all covered by mounds of earth. Excavation of the longest trench revealed that its floor was lined with red ochre and in the middle was a lump of white clay and the spike of a deer antler pushed into the ground. The trench was covered with a thin layer of sand as well as earth.

On top of this, a mound, rising about 30 in (76 cm) high, was made up of several layers. The archaeologists called them 'offering layers', for they contained burned materials, bone spear points and ochre which looked as if they had been part of a burned offering at a religious ceremony. There were also cylinders of mixed earth,

resembling children's sand castles, that had been plastered with coloured clay. One central cylinder was surrounded by six others to form a flower-like rosette. The entire structure was surrounded with yellow clay and small stone slabs, and the top was paved with large slabs and rubble with two hearths positioned on top.

Inside the smallest trench was a lump of red ochre beside a small hollow. Resting on top was a simple sculpture, about 14 in (36 cm) high, made from a stone block with a natural fissure down the centre. Grooves had been cut in the rock that, together with

the rock's natural blemishes, produced what looked like the features of a face, the right half resembling a male human countenance, the left, a cat such as a lynx or lion.

The symbolic representation of the twin aspects of nature – the benign and the wild – is known from modern communities, but

DISASTER REPORT *An eruption of the Icelandic volcano Hekla blanketed the Earth with dust, an event recorded in 3300-year-old Chinese manuscripts.*

is rarely seen in the artefacts of ancient peoples. The human-cat statuette was just one example at El Juyo. Another lay in the contrast between the antler spike and white clay found in the longest trench and the hollow and red ochre in the smallest – the spike representing an opposite to the hollow, the white clay to the red ochre.

It is thought that the walled space containing the trenches was set aside from everyday life. Good tools and weapons, which must have taken some considerable time and effort, not to mention skill, to fashion, were offered to whatever god or supernatural being the ancient people of El Juyo worshipped. This special place, or

MURAL ART *A rock carved with spiral symbols marks the entrance to the 5000-year-old passage grave at Newgrange in Ireland.*

STANDING STONES *About 1000 stones set in rows mark the Kermario alignment, part of a concentration of megaliths at Carnac, France.*

sanctuary, revealed the existence of religious behaviour 14 000 years ago. Why these people should have been drawn to the worship of a supernatural being is unknown. A change of climate and the consequent change in plant and animal life might have caused uncertainty and unrest, creating a need for collective reassurance. Or perhaps religion had a role to play in bringing together different but neighbouring cultures. It could also have been a means by which an elite could control the behaviour of the masses, the threat of supernatural powers providing

insurance against insurrection.

The excavations at El Juyo – together with those at the nearby Altamira caves, where the work of ancient artists decorates the walls and ceilings of chambers that acted as a kind of assembly point for people from neighbouring communities – prove another point: that some kind of civilisation was emerging. Activities were afoot that

were not solely focused on the day-to-day, hand-to-mouth business of survival. Like most episodes in the story of mankind, this development happened over thousands of years.

THE MONUMENT BUILDERS

The most obvious signs of an evolving civilisation are the structures erected by the megalith builders – passage graves, stone circles, standing stones, chamber tombs, long barrows, menhirs and dolmens with names such as Stonehenge, Carnac, Avebury, Barnenez and Maes Howe. The simplest megaliths were the dolmens – three or four pillars supporting a massive capstone – and the most complex were the passage graves, such as the Quanterness tomb in Orkney. This is a circular burial site composed of six-sided chambers, each with a circumference of 148 ft (45 m) and a height of 12 ft (3.7 m). The architects and builders were not the newly emerging metalsmiths and industrialists of the Middle and Near East, but the New Stone Age farmers of northern Europe.

At first, archaeologists thought that the monument builders were simply adopting the fashions of the Middle East and the Mediterranean. This view was the result of inaccurate dating techniques. We now know that the megalithic monuments of northern Europe are nearly 2000 years older than anything in the south. In Brittany, great alignments of standing stones, like those at Carnac, which are ³/₄ mile (1.2 km) long, are estimated to be 6500 years old. The stone circles of Stonehenge, Avebury and the Ring of Brogar in Orkney are more than

FIRST COMMANDMENTS
The King of Babylon receives a
code of laws from the god Shamash.
The relief predates the Ten
Commandments by over 500 years.

4500 years old. But why were they built? What function did they serve?

Most of these extraordinary megaliths took many man-hours to construct, and they were, on one level at least, without any prac-

STONEHENGE *The standing*
stones on England's Salisbury
Plain are observatory, place
of worship and monument to a
wealthy chief combined.
Overleaf: A wall carving
from a Peruvian temple of
1600 BC shows human victims
being sacrificed.

tical function. They were symbolic. Stonehenge, a circle of standing stones linked together by enormous lintels, took an estimated 30 million man-hours to build, and nearby Silbury Hill, a large artificial earth mound – the largest man-made structure in Europe before the Industrial Revolution – took 18 million man-hours. The investment in labour was enormous, and it is thought that 'chiefdom' societies – groups or tribes headed by chiefs – were the necessary stimulus for their construction.

In Britain, the centres of these chiefdoms were marked by megalithic monu-

continued on page 152

ments. First, from 6000 to 5500 years ago, came the constructions known as causewayed camps – circular enclosures surrounded by a series of incomplete concentric ditches protected by a wooden perimeter fence. Later, from about 5000 years ago, came henges, circular enclosures bordered by a ditch and a bank and topped by a wooden or stone edifice. These monuments were surrounded by any number of long barrow burial mounds.

Stonehenge and Silbury Hill were probably the result of some kind of federation of chiefdoms, since no single chiefdom could have achieved such a formidable task. It has

DENUDED DOLMEN *Pentre Ifan in south Wales would originally have been covered with an artificial mound of earth and stone.*

been estimated that Silbury Hill was completed in no more than two years, a schedule which would have needed a team of 3700 men, working eight hours a day for 300 days a year.

Work on Stonehenge got under way about 4500 years ago when a group of farming families gathered on Salisbury Plain, possibly using a hide-rope compass to draw a huge circle. More than 1200 years and 40 generations later the project was finished. Some 3000 years later again, experts are still debating why these people built it. Was it a gigantic status symbol for an alliance of farming communities in southern England trying to impress their neighbours? Was it a religious centre built by the elite to underline their power, or was it perhaps a huge calendar calibrated to align with the sun, moon and stars at various times of the year?

BRITAIN'S OLDEST WOODEN BUILDING

In 1986, archaeologists from Cambridge found what they believe to be the oldest wooden building in the British Isles. It is a wooden burial chamber, measuring 26 ft (8 m) by 6 1/2 ft (1.9 m), and estimated to be between 6000 and 5000 years old. The chamber is contained within a mound of earth, 200 ft (60 m) long – a traditional long barrow – and is made from oak. It was probably the tomb of a wealthy family.

A structure at the other end of the world may hold some clues.

Near Lake Turkana in East Africa a lesser-known megalithic site, Namoratunga II, its

name meaning 'stone people' in the language of the local Turkana people, has been studied by archaeologists and astronomers from Kenya and the USA. The site consists of 19 basaltic pillars, some upright and others leaning to one side.

Turkana legend holds that the pillars, weighing between 99 lb (45 kg) and 550 lb (250 kg) each, are people who were turned to stone by an evil spirit. Science, however, believes them to be a complicated calendar devised by the ancient Cushites about 2300 years ago and still used by the Borana people of southern Ethiopia. The Cushites, who lived close to the fifth cataract of the Nile, were enemies of the Egyptians. They are little understood, for their writing is difficult to decipher.

The Borana people's calendar, like the Maya, Chinese and Hindu ones, is based on the cycles of the Moon and ignores the position of the Sun. It has 354 days and 12 months in a year. Each month lasts 29.5 days – the time the Moon takes to circle the Earth. The start of each month links the Moon with particular star patterns. The start of the year is determined when the new Moon rises with the star Beta Trianguli in the constellation Triangulum. The second month has the new Moon lining up with the Pleiades, and so on through the year. In 1984, when the research was published, New Year's Day, according to this calendar, was on July 28.

The megalithic calendar at Namoratunga II is not far from the Equator and so the relevant stars and the Moon move in an arc directly overhead. The researchers have tried to find ways in which the pillars line up to reflect celestial events in the sky overhead. The stone alignments, according to tests on a Cray computer, one of the most powerful in the world, shows a 99.45 per cent probability that the site is indeed an observation centre.

There has been heated debate about megalithic astronomy, but evidence now suggests that Stone Age man used the mysterious stone circles found all over the world, not just to boost a community's status, but as precise astronomical calculators. Prehistoric man must thus have had a good understanding of the heavens, the stars and the planets. It was the birth of science, a field of endeavour that was to change the natural order of things on the Earth, and to have an extraordinary influence on the next chapters in the story of mankind.

BUILDING THE PYRAMIDS

The world's largest building in 2630 BC was an empty tomb – the Step Pyramid of the Egyptian Pharaoh Djoser. He ordered the construction of this vast monument, which would house him when he died, to inspire reverence in his subjects, to make them think that he was more god-like than human. It rose more than 200 ft (60 m) above the desert floor, and its step shape, with six tiers that decreased in size towards the top, represented a ladder to the heavens which the king would climb to join the gods. Stone was used – rather than the more normal mud-brick, used in houses – to make sure that the edifice would last for ever. Later pharaohs were hugely impressed and, determined not to be outdone, they erected even bigger pyramids. The largest was the Great Pyramid at Giza, measuring 481 ft (147 m) high and 756 ft (230 m) along each side of its square base; it is still one of the largest buildings in the world. The remains of 70 pyramids, all built between 2700 and 100 BC, survive along the banks of the Nile in Egypt and Sudan.

The effort that went into their construction was enormous. Thousands of people would have been co-opted into cutting the rocks, moving the blocks and raising them into place. Cemeteries have been found where the skeletons of hundreds of workers show compressed and damaged vertebrae, the result of many years of carrying heavy loads. Some individuals have fingers and limbs missing. The undertaking would also have required considerable social organisation as well as a mastery of architecture and engineering. A network of canals, for example, was established, which enabled stones and food for the workers to be floated in from the Nile, the main artery of transport through Egypt.

The limestone facing blocks for the Great Pyramid were brought from quarries across the Nile at Tura, and dragged to the work site on sledges pulled by teams of oxen. Ramps of rubble were built against the sides of the emerging pyramid, enabling the stones to be hauled into place. Whether these were single long ramps, with a slope of about one in ten, against each face, or wraparound ramps, supported by the slope of the pyramid itself, is not clear. Scientists today feel that the wraparound ramp was probably used because the single ramp would have been too long to be practical. Archaeologists have also failed to find the necessary amount of rubble that would have been needed to build a ramp against, say, Pharaoh Khufu's Pyramid at Giza. Once up the ramp, the stones would have been lowered into place using a lifting tackle of rope, wood and stone where necessary.

STONE HAULAGE *An Egyptian wall painting shows a team of oxen pulling a sledge to transport large building blocks.*

The desire to impress by building huge monuments has been a regular feature of the world's civilisations. A little later than Djoser of Egypt, from about 2112 to 2095 BC, Ur-Nammu reigned in the city state of Ur in southern Mesopotamia. He built the great Ziggurat of Ur, a vast pyramid-like structure, designed not as a tomb for himself but as a platform for a temple which would thus be

TOMBS OF STONE *The pyramids of Egypt differ from many other ancient monuments in that the stones were carefully shaped and fitted together, and at the centre were tombs.*

MAYAN SPLENDOUR *Mayan pyramids differed from Egyptian ones in that a mound of earth was faced with stone, forming the base of a temple.*

raised towards the heavens. Many hundreds of years later, on the far side of the Atlantic, the Maya people of what is now Mexico and Guatemala also built pyramids that overawed onlookers with a sense of the majesty of the gods and of the priests and their attendants who were allowed to climb them. Like the Ziggurat of Ur, the Mayan pyramids were raised platforms for temples; they were often arranged around enormous ceremonial plazas. They were built from about 1200 BC until AD 1519 when the Spanish conquistadores invaded the New World.

Unlike the Egyptian pyramids, which had square bases and four triangular sides ending in a point, the Mayan ones were flat-topped polyhedrons with bases that were either square or rectangular. One or more staircases, connecting each ascending terrace, led from the base to the flattened top. Unlike Egyptian monuments, which were all of stone, they consisted mainly of mounds of earth faced with stone. They were re-newed, following a complicated calendar system, every 52 years, when another layer of stone was added to the

previous surface all around the pyramid – meaning that they just grew and grew.

The Maya were not the only people of Mexico and Central America to have built pyramids. The oldest was built by the people of the Olmec civilisation which flourished in south-eastern Mexico between 1100 and 800 BC. The largest standing New World pyramid is the 216 ft (66 m) high Pyramid of the Sun, part of a vast ceremonial complex built between AD 300 and 650 at Teoti-

huacán, farther north. This pyramid is about 720 ft by 760 ft (220 m by 230 m) at its base and has 220 steps to the temple plat-form at its top. The sides are less steep than those of Egyptian pyramids, and it is made of volcanic rock which was probably covered with plaster and painted, though the deco-ration is now long gone. Even today, in the age of skyscrapers, the Pyramid of the Sun strikes a sense of awe – as it was designed to – in anyone standing at its foot.

RAMP SYSTEM *The stone for Egyptian pyramids was probably raised either by a straight, inclined ramp (top) or a wraparound ramp (bottom). Both methods had problems. The straight ramp would have had to be constantly built up as the pyramid height increased, while the wraparound ramp had to be supported on the sloping sides of the pyramid.*

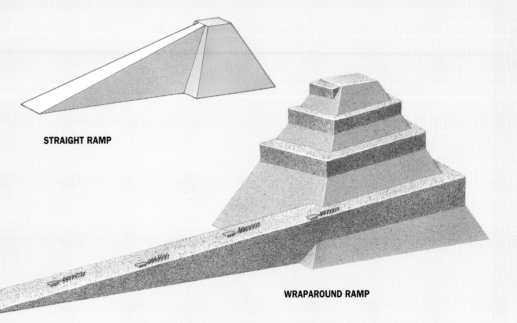

STRAIGHT RAMP

WRAPAROUND RAMP

PICTURE CREDITS

3 OSF/Belinda Wright. **6** BCL/Rod Williams. **7** SPL/Space Telescope Science Institute/NASA. **8** Mary Evans Picture Library, TL; Bodleian Library, Oxford, BM. **9** SPL/John Reader, TM; SPL/John Reader, BR. **10** SPL/Will & Deni McIntyre. **11** Zefa Pictures. **12** Peter Kain © Richard Leakey, TL; OSF/Richard Herrmann, BR. **13** Peter Kain © Richard Leakey, TL; SPL/BSIP, BR. **14** Siena Artworks/Ron Hayward, BL, MR. **15** Siena Artworks/Lorraine Harrison, TL; OSF/Richard Packwood, BR. **16** OSF/Animals, Animals/Raymond A. Mendez, TR; Gerald Cubitt, BL. **17** OSF/Clive Bromhall, MR; Siena Artworks/Ron Hayward, BL. **18** Siena Artworks/Mike Saunders, BR; Siena Artworks/Mike Saunders, MR. **19** Siena Artworks/Lorraine Harrison. **20** Siena Artworks/Ron Hayward, BL; Peter Kain © Richard Leakey, BR. **21** SPL/John Reader, TR; WWI/Nigel Hicks, BL. **22** BCL/R.I.M. Campbell, TR; Siena Artworks/Ron Hayward, BL. **23** OSF/Konrad Wothe. **24** Peter Kain © Richard Leakey, BL; Mary Evans Picture Library, BR. **25** BCL/Gunter Ziesler, TR; Siena Artworks/Ron Hayward, B. **26** Prof. Louis de Bonis, BL. **26-27** OSF/Malcolm Coe. **28** Siena Artworks/Ron Hayward. **29** SPL/John Reader, TL; OSF/Bruce Davidson, TR. **30** OSF/Mark Pidgeon, TL; Siena Artworks/Ron Hayward, BR. **31** WWI/Mike Powles. **32** SPL/John Reader, L; Siena Artworks/Ron Hayward, BL. **33** Institute of Human Origins/Don Johanson, L; SPL/John Reader, TR. **34** Siena Artworks/Malcolm McGregor. **35** SPL/John Reader, TL; Illustrated London News, BL. **36** Peter Kain © Richard Leakey, TR; Siena Artworks/ Christian Hook, B. **37** Werner Forman Archive, TM; Natural History Museum, TR. **38** Siena Artworks/Ron Hayward, inset. **38-39** SPL/John Reader. **40** SPL/John Reader, BL;

National Museums of Kenya, TR. **41** Illustrated London News, MR; Natural History Museum, BR. **42** Siena Artworks/Malcolm McGregor. **43** SPL/John Reader, TL; Peter Kain © Richard Leakey, BR. **44** Siena Artworks/Christian Hook. **45** Siena Artworks/Ron Hayward. **46** OSF/Clive Bromhall, BL; Peter Kain © Richard Leakey, TR. **47** Peter Kain © Richard Leakey. **48** Siena Artworks/Malcolm McGregor. **49** Peter Kain © Richard Leakey, TL; Siena Artworks/Christian Hook, B. **50** SPL/John Reader, T; Peter Kain © Richard Leakey, BL. **51** NHPA/Anthony Bannister. **52** Siena Artworks/Ron Hayward, TL; Peter Kain © Richard Leakey, BL. **53** G. Burenhult Productions. **54** Siena Artworks/Malcolm McGregor **55** SPL/John Reader, TL; Mary Evans Picture Library, BR. **56-57** Siena Artworks/Andy Lloyd-Jones. **58** Peter Kain © Richard Leakey. **59** Siena Artworks/Christian Hook. **60** Siena Artworks/Malcolm McGregor, BL; Siena Artworks/Aldo Balding, BR. **61** SPL/John Reader, TM; Robert Harding Picture Library, B. **62** Auscape International/J.M. Labat, TR; SPL/Astrid & Hanns-Frieder Michler, ML; Auscape International/J.M. Labat, BL, BC, BR; Siena Artworks/Ron Hayward, MR. **63** SPL, BR. **64-65** G. Burenhult Productions. **66** G. Burenhult Productions, TR; National Geographic/Sisse Brimberg, BL. **67** Auscape International/M.W. Gillam, BR, BL. **68** AKG/Erich Lessing. **69** The Hutchison Library/André Singer, TL; Robert Estall Photo Library, BR. **70** Sonia Halliday Photographs. **71** Siena Artworks/Lorraine Harrison. **72** Siena Artworks/Aldo Balding, TR; Dr J H Post, BL. **73** Peter Kain © Richard Leakey. **74** Peter Kain © Richard Leakey. **75** Robert Estall Photo Library, ML; The Hutchison Library/Sarah Errington, TR; The Hutchison Library/N. Durrell-McKenna, MR. **76** B. & C. Alexander. **77** Siena Artworks/Dewey Franklin. **78-79** Siena Artworks/Nik Spender. **80** Ira Block Photography, TL; Warren Morgan, BR. **81** Siena Artworks/Lorraine Harrison, MM; Siena Artworks/Jim Robins, all others.

82 OSF/Richard Herrmann. **83** Siena Artworks/Mark Viney, MR; Siena Artworks/Lorraine Harrison, B. **84** B. Arriaza/Smithsonian Institution, TL; R. Rocha & D. Kendrick-Murdock/Smithsonian Institution, BL. **85** D. Kendrick-Murdock/Smithsonian Institution, TL; B. Arriaza/Smithsonian Institution, BR. **86** Siena Artworks/Christian Hook. **87** Siena Artworks/Lorraine Harrison. **88** OSF/Belinda Jones, TR; Auscape International/D. Parer & E. Parer-Cook, MM; Auscape International/Matt Jones, BL. **89** Auscape International/Reg Morrison. **90** Siena Artworks/Nick Mountain. **91** Auscape International/Reg Morrison. **92-93** Auscape International/J.M. La Roque. **94** Robert Harding Picture Library. **95** Siena Artworks/Lorraine Harrison. **96-97** Siena Artworks/Christian Hook. **98** Siena Artworks/Lorraine Harrison, TL, BR. **99** G.R. Roberts. **100** Peter Crawford. **101** Peter Kain © Richard Leakey TL; Robert Estall Photo Library/David Coulson, BR. **102** Auscape International/Ferrero/Labat. **103** Peter Kain © Richard Leakey, TR; Auscape International/J.M. Labat, BL. **104** Michael Holford, TR, ML; The Ancient Art & Architecture Collection, BM. **105** Michael Holford. **106-107** National Geographic/Sisse Brimberg. **108** The Ancient Art & Architecture Collection. **108-109** AKG/Musée de l'Homme. **110** OSF/Paul Franklin, BL; Robert Estall Photo Library/David Coulson, BR. **111** AKG/Erich Lessing, TL; Peter Kain © Richard Leakey, TR; Auscape International/J.M. Labat, ML. **112** Auscape International/Reg Morrison, TR; OSF/Belinda Wright, BL; Auscape International/Hans & Judy Beste, BM. **113** Auscape International/Jean-Paul Ferrero. **114** Michael Holford. **115** Toucan Books Archive. **116-117** Siena Artworks/Nick Spender **118** Michael Holford. **119** Siena Artworks/Julian Puckett. **120** NHPA/Laurie Campbell, TL; B. & C. Alexander, BM. **121** Mick Sharp Photography, TR; Peter Kain © Richard Leakey, ML; Siena Artworks/Ron Hayward, B.

122-123 Michael Holford. **124** Toucan Books Archive, TL; Siena Artworks/Ron Hayward, B. **125** NHPA/Anthony Bannister. **126** AKG/Erich Lessing. **127** Dr. Simon Davis/Nature Magazine. **128** Michael Holford. **129** The Ancient Art & Architecture Collection, TR: Siena Artworks/Ed Stuart, B. **130-131** British Museum. **132** Peter Kain © Richard Leakey, TL; Michael Holford, B. **133** Simon J.M. Davis, TR, MR; Robert Harding Picture Library, BL. **134** Skyscan. **135** National Museum of Denmark. **136** William MacQuitty Collection, TL, B. **137** William MacQuitty Collection. **138-139** William MacQuitty Collection. **140** Linda Proud, TR; Robert Harding Picture Library, BL. **141** Robert Harding Picture Library, TL; Sonia Halliday Photographs, MR. **142-143** BCL/Andy Price. **144** Ashmolean Museum, Oxford. **145** Michael Holford. **146** Michael Holford. **147** Matts Wibe Lund. **148** Mick Sharp Photography, TR; Event Horizons/David Lyons, B. **149** Robert Harding Picture Library/Adam Woolfit, TR; Michael Holford, BM. **150-151** Elizabeth Baquedano. **152-153** Event Horizons/David Lyons. **154** Elizabeth Baquedano. **155** Elizabeth Baquedano, TR; Siena Artworks/Ed Stuart, BR.

FRONT COVER: SPL/John Reader; OSF/Richard Herrmann, M.

77-010-1